MY FELLOW TEXANS

Governors of Texas
In the 20th Century

Dede W. Casad

EAKIN PRESS ★ **Austin, Texas**

FIRST EDITION

Copyright © 1995
By Dede W. Casad

Published in the United States of America
By Eakin Press
An Imprint of Sunbelt Media, Inc.
P.O. Drawer 90159 ★ Austin, TX 78709-0159

ISBN 0-89015-996-3

10 9 8 7 6 5 4 3 2

Library of Congress Cataloging-in-Publication Data

Casad, Dede W., 1928–
  My fellow Texans : governors of Texas in the 20th century / by Dede W.
Casad.
       p.   cm.
  Includes bibliographical references.
  ISBN 0-89015-996-3 : $12.95
  1. Governors — Texas — Biography — Juvenile literature. 2. Texas —
Politics and government — 1865–1950 — Juvenile literature. 3. Texas —
Politics and government — 1951– — Juvenile literature. I. Title.
F385.C37   1995
976.4'06'0922 -- dc20
[B]   94-21991
                                                                    CIP
                                                                    AC

*To eight native Texans who will help govern
The Lone Star State in the 21st century.*

*Victor McCrae, Carter Summerfield, Christopher Miles,
Matthew Grant, Andrew Alexander, Mitchell Gordon,
Katherine Reeves, and Scott Thomas.*

SAM HOUSTON, Texas' First Governor
— From a portrait by William Henry Hurdle in the Texas State Capitol.
Courtesy Texas State Library.

CONTENTS

AUTHOR'S NOTE

The quotations preceding each governor's biographical sketch are taken directly from one of their inaugural addresses.

The dates designated under their names are the dates spanning their complete terms.

Joseph Draper Sayers

*It should be known everywhere that in no other
state is life, liberty and property so secure; in no
other state are offenses against them so surely, so
speedily and so sufficiently punished; and in no
other state is such complete justice between all men
as to all kinds of property maintained as within the
great Commonwealth of Texas.*

*. . . An empire in extent, resources almost
limitless, situation altogether favorable, and an
open sea around her southern border, Texas may
well aspire to a greatness and grandeur that will
have no parallel in the history and experience of
her sister states.*

Joseph Draper Sayers
1899

JOSEPH DRAPER SAYERS

The twentieth century emerged in the state of Texas with Joseph Draper Sayers sitting in the governor's seat. His term began without serious event, but ended dramatically.

The boll weevil beetle hit Texas, destroying farm crops. And on the morning of September 8, 1900, the worst hurricane in Texas' history lashed out at the city of Galveston. Winds blew up to 120 miles per hour, and the tidal wave rose to six feet. Between six thousand and eight thousand people were killed, and the city was totally destroyed.

Governor Sayers rushed to petition Congress for disaster relief. He immediately requested ten thousand tents and fifty thousand ration packages from the army. The food arrived but only one thousand tents came. The Red Cross, headed by Clara Barton, marshaled its resources, then headed for Texas to attend to the survivors. More than forty thousand dollars a day was spent on relief for the families of over twelve thousand Texans.

The disaster caught the attention of the entire nation. President and Mrs. William McKinley came to Texas at the invitation of Governor Sayers to view the damage. Unfortunately, four months later the president was assassinated.

Gov. "Joe" Sayers was the first governor to involve the national government in a state's disaster. Another notable event during his administration occurred when the legislature passed a law making it necessary for Texans to pay a tax to vote. This is the poll tax that we have today.

Governor Sayers is also remembered as the governor

2

of the oil industry. It was in 1901 that the Lucas Gusher struck oil at Spindletop, and Texas and America entered the oil age.

Joseph Draper Sayers was born in Grenada, Mississippi, of Celtic parents on September 23, 1841. His mother died when he was young. Heartbroken, father and young Joe, who was ten years old, moved to Bastrop, Texas.

In 1852 Joe's father enrolled him in the Bastrop Military Institute to assure a good, formal education. However, life was to educate him in a practical way, for the Civil War was brewing. Young Joe joined the Confederate Army as a private when he was nineteen.

A fighter at heart, Joe Sayers was equipped for the war zone. Within a year, he was commissioned captain in the Confederate Army; then he rapidly rose to the rank of major.

But all was not bugles and flashy uniforms on the field of battle. Sayers was wounded twice during the war. The second wound occurred when a bullet ripped through his leg just above the ankle. Determined to stay with his men, he ordered crutches and returned to the front line.

When the war was over, Joe Sayers returned to Bastrop and began teaching school. Always wanting to better himself, he began studying law at night.

He married Ada Walton in 1868. Unfortunately, she died in four short years. Sayers then married Ada's sister, Orline Walton.

Sayers passed the bar in 1866, and after practicing law, he became a member of the state legislature in 1873. In 1878, he became lieutenant governor, but it was twenty long years before he was to reach his coveted goal of becoming governor.

To stay in the political arena, he ran and was elected to Congress in 1885. Sayers served as a congressman until he was finally inaugurated as governor of Texas on January 17, 1899.

There is probably no native Texan who could have carried the state from a wilderness to an empire as did

3

Joseph D. Sayers. Texas was experiencing phenomenal growth. The population had reached three million, a third of whom had arrived in the last ten years. As a non-native Texan, himself, he understood the allure of this enchanting state. More importantly, he understood the link between the romantic and primitive life of Texas, as represented by the nineteenth century, and the magnificent development and raw opportunity of Texas, as represented by the twentieth century. He told a Dallas news reporter:

> I have forty-seven years in this state. I came here a bare-footed boy, before a mile of railroad or telegraph line was constructed and I could have bought, if I had had the money, every foot of ground upon which Dallas now stands at twenty-five cents per acre.

After serving two terms as governor of Texas, Joseph Draper Sayers retired to San Antonio to practice law. He died May 15, 1929, in Austin, and is buried in his hometown of Bastrop.

TEXAS TRIVIA AND TRUTH

At this time the bluebonnet was named the state flower. It was also called buffalo clover or wolf clover.

Samuel Willis Tucker Lanham

To attain equal and exact justice to all men, the law must permit equal opportunity to all men, and grant "exclusive privilege to none." The same avenues must be open to all. "Monopoly" say our Constitution, "is contrary to the genius of a free government. Competition is inseparable from free and healthy commerce."

. . . Let no honest investor hesitate to bring and employ his capital in our midst, let every such comer be cordially welcomed and duly protected — let no useful enterprise be intimidated — let industry and legitimate development of all kinds be invited, encouraged and conserved — let prosperity along all rightful lines be hailed, stimulated and advanced, but let the world know that there is more in this state than spoilation.

Samuel Willis Tucker Lanham
1903

SAMUEL WILLIS TUCKER LANHAM

JANUARY 20, 1903 TO JANUARY 15, 1907

In 1901, "Black Gold" was a phrase every Texan knew. After the Lucas Gusher "blew," producing more oil in ten days than the Corsicana field had produced in four years, the oil boom was on. Investors and oil workers flocked to Beaumont. Oil fields, with their strange looking derricks, began to dot the landscape. Jobs were created. New towns were established. Roads were built, and pipelines were laid to accommodate the new industry. Texas was becoming rich fast.

And Texas would never be the same.

The Wild West suddenly turned into a wild scramble for a piece of the action. Though most Texans continued their cotton farming, they hoped that Black Gold would be discovered under their land.

S. W. T. Lanham, elected as governor in 1902, had his hands full. The state of Texas had to meet the challenges its own resources demanded.

With population and state income on the rise, there was both the need and the ability to build new schools. No one realized the need for education more than Governor Lanham. Known as a self-educated man, Governor Lanham, remembered his own lack of schooling.

Neither Texas born nor Texas raised, he was a son of South Carolina and a follower of John C. Calhoun. Calhoun believed strongly in state's rights, that is, the right of every state to govern itself. Lanham held to this belief his entire life.

Lanham was a boy of fifteen when he joined the Confederate Army after the fall of Fort Sumptor. He was wounded at Spotsylvania and was part of the surrendering forces at Greensboro, North Carolina.

After the signing of a peace treaty at Appomattox, Lanham and his family headed for Texas. They settled in the outpost of Parker County, at what is now Weatherford. Lanham studied law and was admitted to the bar in 1869. Shortly thereafter E. J. Davis appointed him attorney for the "jumbo" district. This was a district that stretched from Weatherford to El Paso, some 120,000 square miles. He referred to his vast territory as "bounded on the west by the Grace of God." It covered eighty-three counties.

In 1882, Lanham was elected to Congress from his "jumbo" district. After serving for ten years in Washington, he resigned and returned to Parker County, where he attempted to win the 1894 Democratic gubernatorial nomination. The convention chose Charles Culberson over Lanham. Returning to Congress in 1896, Lanham served three terms before he was nominated to succeed Gov. Joseph Sayers.

Lanham's two terms as governor can be characterized as "homework" years. Texas was at peace. The oil boom was bringing in new and exciting businesses. This allowed the legislature time to attend to some housekeeping chores. An important election law, called the Terrell Election Law of 1903, was enacted. For the first time in Texas, governmental officials were elected by ballot. And for the first time, the citizens went to a voting booth. Voting qualifications were established, and a uniform method of holding primaries was set up.

Samuel Lanham, the last Confederate to serve as governor, came to his job as an elderly man. He had served his country nobly as a congressman, but he believed that the office of the governor had aged him and broken his spirit. He often regretted taking the job. One of the last things he said as he departed the Capitol steps was:

7

I was very happy for years and years seeing the people in my district as their congressional representative. Then I became governor. Office-seekers, pardon-seekers, and concession-seekers overwhelmed me. They broke my health and when a man finds his health gone, his spirit is broken.

Lanham died a sad and dejected man on July 29, 1908. He never recovered the positive attitude of his days as a gallant soldier and faithful public servant.

TEXAS TRIVIA AND TRUTH

The University of Texas performed "The Eyes of Texas" for the first time in a minstrel show.

Thomas Mitchell Campbell

Uphold the Constitution, stand by the platform demands, equalize the burden of government, sweep from these representatives halls the "shoulder clapper" and the hired lobby, strike down the corruptionist and the enemies of the people's government, by precept and example promote economy and civil righteousness and you will earn and receive the approval and the praise of a just and grateful people.

Thomas Mitchell Campbell
1907

THOMAS MITCHELL CAMPBELL

JANUARY 15, 1907 TO JANUARY 19, 1911

"Change" is the word that best describes T. M. Campbell's term as governor. He was called a Progressive governor because he believed in change, or reform, as they called it in those days. Progressives wanted government to be fair. Many people of all races, religions, and economic backgrounds were coming to Texas. The Progressives wanted to serve all the people rather than just the rich and a select few.

Campbell believed that if citizens were to be taxed, they should be taxed equally. He called this tax the Full-Rendition Act. Because farmers did not think it was fair to be taxed like the oil people, many of them became his enemies.

Campbell was also a Prohibitionist. He favored laws regulating liquor. Not only did he want to change liquor laws, he also wanted to regulate lobbyists. Lobbyists were people who were paid by certain groups to influence the lawmakers. Campbell lashed out at them publicly. He called them "shoulder clappers." Campbell was unsuccessful in eliminating lobbyists — we still have them to this day.

Thomas M. Campbell was the second governor to be born in Texas. A native of Palestine, in East Texas, Campbell was known for being wise. They called him the "Sage of Palestine."

His boyhood friend was former governor Jim Hogg. Both men vowed as boys to become governor. Both men did.

As a young man, Tom Campbell attended the Rusk

Masonic Institute. Later he spent one year at Trinity University in Tehuacana, Texas, but had to quit school because his family ran out of money.

Tom got a job working in the district clerk's office in Longview. He studied law at night and soon passed the bar. When someone was looking for Tom, his mother used to say, "Go to the courthouse. You'll find Tom there listening to the lawyer's speak."

It is said that Campbell had two ambitions: one was to become governor of Texas. The other, was to be true to his friends. As Teddy Roosevelt said: "Character, in the long run, is the decisive factor in the life of an individual and of nations alike."

Thomas Campbell exhibited his character throughout his career. Since he had held no other political office before declaring his intentions to become governor, Campbell faced strong opposition in the primary. He had three opponents, M. M. Brooks, O. B. Colquitt, and Charles K. Bell.

At one point in the convention, it appeared that Campbell was not going to win. Sen. Joseph Weldon Bailey, who had been supporting someone else, decided to support Campbell. He got up to speak. As an eloquent orator, he ended his passionate speech with a story. The story was about the siege of Lucknow in the Sepoy Rebellion in India in 1857. He told how a Scottish lassie urged the British defenders to hold out a little longer. They did, and when the bagpipes of the advancing Highlanders were heard, she shouted, "The Campbells are coming."

The tide turned. The convention made the connection between the Lucknow story and the nomination of Thomas Campbell. Immediately, a convention spokesman shouted, "First in the Primary, first in the convention, now let's make it unanimous." Thomas Campbell was their man.

Campbell easily defeated his Republican opponent, and in two years he won the nomination and the election for his second term hands down.

Campbell succeeded in accomplishing several major advancements for his state. He helped pass a pure food law. He strengthened the state's antitrust laws, and he set up major prison reform. He was particularly proud of the fact that he established the Texas State Library.

After his second term as governor, Campbell ran for the Senate. He lost and never ran for a public office again. He died of leukemia on April 1, 1923, in Galveston and was buried in his hometown of Palestine.

TEXAS TRIVIA AND TRUTH

The town of Post, founded by C. W. Post of "Post Toasties" became the county seat of Garza County.

Oscar Branch Colquitt

. . . I stand myself for the progress which means development, for that progress which means the betterment of each individual citizen, and shall ask you . . . to join me in establishing the best system of education of any State in the American nation. I shall ask you to cooperate with me in building the best University controlled by our State . . . join hands with me in making the Agricultural and Mechanical College the best of its kind in the United States. And . . . in the development of the state normal schools and of the College of Industrial Arts for Women: and . . . in each community of the State of Texas to make of themselves the best system of public schools in the United States.

Oscar Branch Colquitt
1913

OSCAR BRANCH COLQUITT

JANUARY 17, 1911 TO JANUARY 19, 1915

In 1910 two issues divided families, townships, and big business — Prohibition and prison brutality.

Even the Democratic party was divided. While campaigning for governor, Oscar Colquitt said at a meeting in Dallas, "We have only one political party in Texas, but there are enough . . . fights in that one for half a dozen."

According to their view of Prohibition, all political candidates were classified as "wets" or "drys." Their political fate would be determined by the final vote on this issue. Oscar B. Colquitt, well-known for his stand against any form of Prohibition, was nominated. What followed was one of the most fervent races for governor in Texas' history. Four heavy contenders battled for the post, but Colquitt came out the winner.

Born December 16, 1861, in Georgia, Oscar Colquitt boasted of humble beginnings. Though his uncle, Alfred H. Colquitt, was a former governor and former senator, his father was an impoverished Confederate veteran.

As a young man Oscar Colquitt and his family moved to Morris County and settled in Dangerfield where he started school. Since his family needed money, Colquitt quit school after five months and worked as a tenant farmer. The rest of his education was self-taught. He read at night after working all day to support his family. In addition to farming, he worked as a porter for the railroad, a furniture mill lineman, and as a printer's apprentice for the Morris County *Banner*.

Young Colquitt had two ambitions — to own his own newspaper and to become a lawyer.

In 1884, after saving $175 from his various jobs, he started the *Pittsburgh Gazette*. Later he sold the *Gazette* to his brother, and started another paper in Terrell, Texas. Colquitt had achieved his first goal.

Privately, Colquitt read every law book he could get his hands on. In 1900 he was admitted to the bar. After he passed the bar, he decided to merge the two papers, and allow his brother to run them. Colquitt began his law practice in Terrell; he had achieved his second goal.

Four years later, he ran for the state Senate, and six years after that, he ran for governor against Thomas Campbell. Colquitt lost the initial race, but tried again after Campbell had served two terms.

Running as an anti-Prohibitionist, Colquitt was known as Oscar "Budweiser" Colquitt. Against statewide Prohibition, he acquiesced to local options, where local communities could decide for themselves, to soothe his opponents.

The election was hard fought and hard won. With 167 counties dry, sixty-one counties partially wet, and twenty-one total wet, it appeared that the "drys" would win. However, the larger voting public lived in the wet counties. Though the election drew more than twice the votes of previous elections, the "wets" won by a slender margin.

If elected, Colquitt had promised to work on prison reform, and he was very dramatic in carrying out his promise. One day, after he was elected, he brought a "bull bat" to the legislative floor. This was a whip-type weapon made of three-inch strips of leather nailed to a large, wooden handle.

A mock trial was staged. A man lay on the Senate floor. Colquitt, a slight man, resembling a modern day Napoleon, had much difficulty wielding the five-foot whip. But he lashed out at the man on the floor to demonstrate the brutality of the "bat." He made his point. Legislation outlawing such abuse in the prison system was enacted. Other changes to the prison system included the abolishment of the practice of leasing convicts for labor outside the prisons and the wearing of striped uniforms. Additionally, sanitation and medical services were improved, and each convict was to be paid a small wage for his labor.

Political issues were not the only thing that plagued the governor. Bands of irate Mexicans had begun to invade Texas. A revolution was breaking out on the Mexican border. Colquitt asked Washington for arms and men to protect the Texas borders. None arrived. Dissatisfied with Washington's neglect, Colquitt sent the Texas Rangers to meet and order the Mexicans to leave or face the consequences. The Mexicans did not retreat willingly, and tension continued to mount between the Colquitt and the Wilson administration.

A small, dynamic man, Colquitt's friends liked to call him "Little Oscar." His enemies were not so kind. They called him the "Napoleon of Texas Politics."

As a self-made man Colquitt was known to be obstinate and hard to deal with. Although he was a handsome man, he lacked the polish of one highly educated. Nevertheless, he was affable, colorful, and memorable.

Before his death on March 8, 1940, he worked for the Reconstruction Finance Corporation.

TEXAS TRIVIA AND TRUTH

Lightenin' Hopkins of blues fame was born in Centerville, Texas, March 15, 1912.

Portrait by G. M. Deane
Eric Beggs, Photographer
State Preservation Board, Austin, TX

James Edward Ferguson

*Prosperity must depend on the condition of labor
and its reward. From the farm, the ranch, and
the workshop come pure-hearted patriots. So
every legitimate effort which tends to lighten the
burdens of industry and create new life therein
should receive our support and commendation.
We should remember that all honest wealth is
the result of labor.*

James Edward Ferguson
1917

JAMES EDWARD FERGUSON

JANUARY 19, 1915 TO AUGUST 25, 1917

The winds of war were blowing across the Atlantic. Europe was setting the stage for a major world conflict. President Wilson was seeking to keep America neutral, and Texans were divided in their patriotism. Some wanted Wilson to declare war and join the Allies. Others, just as fervently, wanted American to stay at home and let the Europeans settle their own disputes.

Texas, however, was about to wage a war of its own. The Progressives, while in office, had made many changes to accommodate a growing state. Industry was expanding, and new businesses were coming to Texas. But no one was paying attention to the farmer.

Enter James Edward Ferguson, a nonpolitical personality, who decided to represent the farmer and his problems. Never having run for public office before, Ferguson was not well-known.

Born in 1871, near Salado in Bell County, to a hard working, poor farmer, Ferguson was a typical farm boy. He worked on the farm until the age of sixteen. Then he left home and went to California. For two years he worked a dozen different jobs, migrating from the West Coast to Nevada to Colorado and finally settling down in Texas on the farm.

Always wanting to advance his education, he began to study law, and without even taking the bar exam, he was licensed to practice.

While working to gain a decent law practice, Ferguson became involved in other business interests — real estate, insurance, and banking. He soon moved to Temple, where he helped start the Temple State Bank.

Gaining local popularity in Temple as a businessman, he announced, in November 1913, that he would be a candidate for governor the next year. This was a surprise to everyone.

"Farmer Jim," had no political party behind him — he had not been nominated. No financial backing was offered. He was running on his own.

The farmers and the tenant class looked upon this favorably. He was unpretentious and made friends easily — traits that held him in good stead.

Thinking that people were sick and tired of hearing about Prohibition, he announced two campaign proposals. If elected governor, he would limit tenants' rents and veto any legislation pertaining to the controversial Prohibition issue.

Fergusons promise to limit tenant farmer rents drew widespread attention. It was a new issue, and reporters began to write about it. The *London Times* devoted prime space in a Sunday issue analyzing his platform and prospects of success. This was among the first of a long line of publicity written about Jim Ferguson. And he loved it. He craved the publicity that politics offered.

Thomas H. Ball of Houston was nominated as Ferguson's opponent, by the Prohibitionists in a convention at El Paso. Ball was well-known, having served in several state offices prior to his nomination. The professional politician didn't give Ferguson a chance.

The election proved to be a hot one. Tempers flared as Ferguson, "The People Candidate" or "The Peanut Candidate" stood his ground against Bell's plan for a "saloonless nation."

On election day most Texans were stunned. Against the combined forces of the state's leading politicians and the president of the United States, Ferguson won.

Jim Ferguson's first administration went well. Many

laws were passed. A farm bill limiting rent on Texas farms was accepted. A rural school aid bill also passed, specifying that, in order to qualify for aid, the school district should first levy a local school tax. Funds for rural schools were immediately forthcoming. Texans were pleased with their governor.

His second term, however, was not so successful. Ferguson's opponent in the second race was Charles H. Morris, a wealthy banker from East Texas. After the election, with revenge in mind, Morris charged that Ferguson had used state funds for personal expenses, and his campaign had been financed by a Houston brewery. Morris also alleged that Ferguson had collected the insurance money, some $100,000, on a school destroyed by fire. Then put the money in his Temple bank and refused to pay to the state interest due on the use of that money.

Ferguson denied all charges. But the fight was on. Ferguson further injured himself politically when he and some officials of the University of Texas had a disagreement. Ferguson demanded that the president of the university be fired, along with several members of the Board of Regents, or else he would veto the university's entire appropriation bill.

A campaign to impeach Ferguson began.

Since Ferguson refused to call a special session of the legislature to hear the charges against himself, the Speaker of the House did. A special investigation committee was appointed and soon the House voted for impeachment.

Ferguson resigned a day before the impeachment took place.

Although he was thrown out of office, Ferguson was not out of politics. After he launched an unsuccessful bid for the United States Senate, he returned to Temple. There he founded the *Ferguson Forum,* a small newspaper, which he used as a weapon against his enemies for the next twenty years.

Never discouraged, "Farmer Jim" resigned himself to helping his wife, Miriam Ferguson, during her two separate terms as governor of Texas.

TEXAS TRIVIA AND TRUTH

Rice University and Baylor University play basketball for the first time, setting up the Southwest Conference.

William Pettus Hobby

Looking forward, my countrymen, there is cause for congratulation in the brighter view that binds our nation and our state by the ties of a grandeur destiny. While the future, whose magnitude and whose promise could only have been dreamed of in years gone by, is now unfolding before us a living and actual reality, the silver lining beyond the war clouds is plainly visible on the horizon of Texas.

William Pettus Hobby
1919

WILLIAM PETTUS HOBBY

SEPTEMBER 26, 1917 TO JANUARY 18, 1921

By 1915 the Petticoat Lobby, a women's organization, was armed for war much like America was armed for war against Europe. Women wanted to vote. Suffrage groups were organized and ready to submit a constitutional amendment to the legislature.

The United States had entered World War I. Texans were enthusiastically supporting the war. Young men were drafted. Large training camps were established throughout the state, and for the first time, air bases came to Texas.

After the impeachment of Governor Ferguson, William Pettus Hobby was sworn in as governor of Texas. Ferguson had been formally impeached the day before, making the transfer of leadership extremely awkward. In addition to the Ferguson scandal, huge state problems awaited this young reporter turned governor.

Will Hobby was born in Moscow, Texas, in 1878, but he moved to Houston at an early age. Next door to the public high school he attended in Houston was the office of the *Houston Post*. Every day Will would stop by and talk to the reporters.

At the age of sixteen, he quit school to work for the paper. He started as a clerk in the circulation department, then rose rapidly to reporter, and two years later became the youngest managing editor in the history of that newspaper.

The *Beaumont Enterprise* took note and invited him to move to their city and become the publisher and editor of the *Enterprise.* He took their offer, and in Beaumont he gained popularity as a leader in the successful drive to build a channel between Beaumont and the Gulf of Mexico, making Beaumont a deep-water port.

In 1914, his friends encouraged him to enter the race for lieutenant governor. He won his first and second election with James Ferguson as his running mate.

When Ferguson faltered, Will Hobby, unexpectedly, found himself the chief executive officer of Texas, a state with many problems. Texas had suffered a prolonged drought; pink bollworms were threatening the cotton industry, and the Prohibition issue had not been put to rest. Women were demanding the ballot, and the fear of German submarines reported near Galveston had reached hysterical proportions. Additionally, there were many state obligations relating to the war effort.

This short, unpretentious, never spectacular man, quietly went about his job with fairness and dignity. Hobby's first action in office was to sign a bill giving women the right to vote. Because of the need for servicemen to be transported quickly, he immediately set up a Highway Department with a mandate to build new roads and improve old roads. More than 200,000 young men were now stationed in Texas. This represented one-seventh of all American servicemen.

This youthful governor weathered the war years admirably, and afterwards he decided to seek a second term. Ironically, it was Jim Ferguson, the impeached governor, who ran against him.

Ferguson had always been fond of making fun of the young Hobby. He scoffed at his large ears and his small stature. Not to be ridiculed without a fight, Hobby returned the jokes. He said, "I will admit that the Supreme Being failed to favor me with physical attributes pleasing to Governor Ferguson but at least He gave me the intelligence to know the difference between my own money and that which belongs to the State." Hobby won the election with twice as many votes as Ferguson.

Education was high on Hobby's list of concerns. With legislative cooperation, a law was passed to supplement the available school funds for the purpose of raising the salaries of public schoolteachers. A tax on oil production was levied, and a state board of control, that is a central purchasing agency, was authorized.

The most important of all Governor Hobby's programs was women's suffrage. Women from all parts of Texas had convinced Governor Hobby that it was time for the women to vote. On March 26, 1918, a law permitting women to vote in primary elections and at political conventions was signed. They still could not vote in the general elections. Then in August of 1920, the Nineteenth Amendment was ratified, and women across the United States were allowed to vote in all elections.

The Texas Equal Suffrage Association became the Texas League of Women Voters. This organization is still active.

After three and a half years in the Governor's Mansion, Hobby went back to Beaumont and to his newspaper. Soon he rejoined the *Houston Post* and never entered politics again.

Governor Hobby married Willie Chapman Cooper in 1915. She died after fourteen years of marriage. Hobby then married Oveta Culp, a former parliamentarian of the House of Representatives. Mrs. Hobby achieved the rank of colonel in the army and was the first Secretary of Health, Education and Welfare, under Eisenhower.

Will Hobby finally bought the *Houston Post* in 1939, and in 1955 his wife became its president.

Governor Hobby died in Houston on June 7, 1964, nine years before his son, Bill, became lieutenant governor.

TEXAS TRIVIA AND TRUTH

Neiman Marcus, an internationally known store, opened September 8, 1907.

Pat Morris Neff

I know the people of Texas. I have recently met them face to face in the fields, the forests, and the factories. I have mixed and mingled with them on the roadside and at the fireside from the banks of the Red River to the Rio Grande, from the plains of the Panhandle to the pines of East Texas, and I am here to bear witness that we will not represent the citizenship of this State if we do not feel the thrill and the throb of that consciously growing pulse beat of the people for that fine, high type of civilization which countenances no dishonesty in private thinking, no camouflage in social life, and no double-dealing in public service. We are here to direct the destinies, to lift the ideals, to make and administer the laws, to protect the weak and curb the greed of the strong, to perpetuate the liberty, to guarantee the industrial freedom of five million people.

Pat Morris Neff
1921

PAT MORRIS NEFF

With the end of the war, patriotism was high, and a new "invisible empire" began to spread throughout the state. The Ku Klux Klan had migrated from Georgia to Texas. They declared their purpose to be "the preservation of law and order, protection of virtuous womanhood and orthodox Protestant moral standards, abstinence from alcoholic beverages, premarital chastity, marital fidelity, respect for parental authority, and maintenance of white supremacy."

The Klan first appeared in Texas in October 1920. They were dressed in their hooded attire and marched in a Confederate veterans' parade in Houston. They announced they would make war on corruption wherever they found it. Their good intentions were negated by their practices. Using threats and violence, they would run "sinners" out of town. The KKK became powerful enough to take the law into their own hands.

As governor, Pat Neff found himself swimming in a sea of troubled waters. Following a mild, but effective man, Pat Neff, the twenty-eighth governor, faced a difficult task. He needed to establish order and control violence.

Pat Neff was a native of McGregor, a small community near Waco. After receiving his B.A. from Baylor University, he attended the law school at the University of Texas. Neff was always interested in politics. As a young attorney of twenty-nine, he was elected to the legislature, and in three more years he was elected Speaker of the House.

After five years, Pat returned to Waco and served

McLennan County as its prosecuting attorney. Highly effective, he lost only sixteen of 422 criminal cases.

Often compared to Woodrow Wilson in looks and demeanor, Neff set up his gubernatorial campaign with a pro-Wilson platform. Unfortunately, Wilson had many political opponents in Texas. The loudest and most popular opponent was Joseph Weldon Bailey. Bailey entered the primaries with strong support. Two other candidates ran against him but the fight was mainly between those that championed the Wilson platform, and those that did not. Bailey won the run-off.

Now with the candidates narrowed to two, the issues were clear. Bailey was for cutting state expenditures, reducing taxes, improving education facilities, separating church and state, and decreasing control from Washington. He denounced labor unions, national Prohibition, women's suffrage, the League of Nations, socialism, monopolies, and class legislation. Neff, on the other hand, favored woman's suffrage, national Prohibition, strict law enforcement, fewer pardons for criminals, higher teacher salaries, and nine-month school terms. Neff was particularly interested in building better highways and state parks. He accused Bailey of not entering the twentieth century. And Bailey, in turn, accused Neff of destroying the time-honored principles of democracy.

Pat Neff was elected governor largely due to his close association with the people of Texas. He campaigned in his own car, driving from township to township. He was the first governor to take an airplane to distant places during his campaign.

After the election, Neff's immediate concern was stopping the violence that the Klan members had instigated. Neff wanted strict law enforcement measures taken against any police officer who was found delinquent in his duties. But the legislature was not cooperative. They felt Neff, a dedicated Baptist, exhibited too high a moral tone for the good of the state.

Yet, Neff worked to keep his campaign promises.

Having sent many criminals to the penitentiary as a prosecutor, Neff was tough on crime. He abolished the pardon board and corrected abuses in the prison system. He called upon lawmakers to pass a system of state parks and playgrounds. He approved large appropriations for education.

Neff's second term was mostly spent making speeches. He appealed to the people to make Texas a manufacturing state. He also encouraged scientific endeavors. Neff was in favor of Texas money staying in Texas.

Pat Neff was a handsome man and a great orator. Some thought he was austere and cold, while others considered his demeanor dignified and reserved. His roommate at Baylor University, Samuel P. Brooks, said of him, "Strange, to say, though Texan born and a rustic, to this day he has never shot a gun, baited a fish hook, used tobacco in any form, nor drunk anything stronger than Brazos water. He does not know one card from another and cannot play any kind of a social game."

After his term was over, Neff went back to Waco to study law. He was elected president of the University of Texas by the Board of Regents, but Neff refused the invitation. In 1932 he accepted the presidency of Baylor University. The Pat Neff Hall stands today as a memorial of his efforts at Baylor.

Pat Neff died in Waco on January 20, 1952. His wife, Myrtle Mainer Neff of Loveland, Texas, died the following year.

TEXAS TRIVIA AND TRUTH

The highest point in Texas is the top of Guadalupe Peak, 8,751 feet in Culberson County.

Miriam Amanda Ferguson

The people have spoken. Their verdict is plain. Their edict is that this must be a government of law founded on the sacred constitution handed down to us by our fathers and mothers of the pioneer days. To this end let us reconsecrate our lives and all that we possess.

. . . As the first woman governor of our beloved State, I ask for the good will and the prayers of the women of Texas. I want to be worthy of the trust and confidence which they have reposed in me.

Miriam Amanda Ferguson
1925

MIRIAM AMANDA FERGUSON

JANUARY 20, 1925 TO JANUARY 17, 1927

&

JANUARY 17, 1933 TO JANUARY 15, 1935

By the midtwenties, the Ku Klux Klan had gained a strong and violent hold in Texas. Admittedly a secret organization, its members, only white Anglo males, wore white hooded robes to hide their identity. They had two basic goals: to remove Catholics, Jews, and African Americans from Texas, and to seize political power.

In order to accomplish their first task, they burned crosses in the lawns of "unacceptable" people, and often tarred and feathered "immoral" people, who they determined were not true Americans.

To accomplish their second goal, the KKK supported certain candidates for office by funding most of their campaign. They controlled law enforcement by supporting their own members as sheriffs and judges, and by electing those who were sympathetic to their cause. During these years, the KKK succeeded in electing a Klansman, Earl B. Mayfield, as a senator.

Now that Pat Neff's term as governor was at an end, the Klan supported Judge Felix Robertson as a candidate. Jim Ferguson was also a candidate. The pro-Ferguson legislators unsuccessfully attempted to get the impeachment proceeding removed from the record. The impeachment record was not erased, and "Farmer Jim" was denied the right to hold public office.

But "Farmer Jim" was not to be silenced. In his newspaper the *Ferguson Forum,* he announced that a Ferguson would be on the ballot. To everyone's surprise,

Jim Ferguson placed his wife, Miriam Amanda Ferguson, on the ballot.

Few women were in politics at the time. Women had only recently received the right to vote. Mrs. Ferguson took advantage of this fact and appealed to the female voter.

Not one for eloquent speeches, Mrs. Ferguson would campaign with her husband. She would make a few opening remarks then turn the podium over to her husband, who would make an impassioned speech opposing the Klan or the "hooded riders" as he called them. In response to the charge that Mrs. Ferguson would only be a figurehead if elected, Jim Ferguson would slyly say, "Two governors for the price of one."

"Ma" and "Pa" Ferguson, as they became known, were the first "team" governorship in the country.

Mrs. Ferguson won both the primary and the general election by a large majority and became the first woman governor in the United States.

Miriam Amanda Wallace Ferguson was born June 13, 1875, to a wealthy family in Bell County. She attended Salado College and Baylor Female College in Belton. Though a large woman, she was stately in manner and smart in dress. Her hat collection was famous. One of her campaign slogans was "Sunbonnet or the Hood."

Governor Ferguson immediately asked the legislature to pass a law outlawing masks in public. This was a positive step in ending the secret activities of the Klan.

Her second move was to decrease population in the penitentiaries. They were overcrowded with prisoners charged with "bootlegging." In record time, Mrs. Ferguson had pardoned over two thousand inmates.

The State Highway Commission posed a problem for the Fergusons. The public accused the Fergusons of signing state contracts only with construction companies who had voted for them. Ironically Jim Ferguson was a member of that commission. Some said that construction companies had to buy advertising space in *Ferguson Forum* in order to be considered for a job with the state. It was soon common knowledge that to get what one wanted from the state government one had to polish the Ferguson apple.

When the time came for reelection, Ma Ferguson was once again on the ballot. But when Dan Moody, who was an even stronger anti-Klan spokesman, announced his candidacy, many people switched their support and voted for him.

However, Miriam Ferguson was to have a comeback. In 1933, after losing two elections (the first against Dan Moody and the second against Ross Sterling) she returned to the governor's seat. This time, she ran on the concept of change. Texas had suffered miserably from the Depression and a severe drought. Sterling was perceived to be the "big business" governor, and again the farmers were left out. Texans wanted change.

Ma Ferguson won her second term by a slim margin, and her tenure as governor was difficult. She proposed a sales tax to help the farmers, but it failed to pass the legislature. She also proposed a corporate income tax, but the legislature passed a tax only on the value of oil.

It was during her second term that she seriously dealt with the economy. She closed banks across the state, paralyzing the economy.

This time when Ma Ferguson left the Governor's Mansion, she never returned. She stayed politically involved and always supported Democratic candidates. Jim Ferguson died in 1944; Miriam Ferguson died on June 25, 1961, and was buried beside her husband in the Texas State Cemetery in Austin.

TEXAS TRIVIA AND TRUTH

"So Long, It's Been Good to Know You," was written by Woody Guthrie to memorialize the dislocation of West Texas farmers due to the Dust Bowl.

Portrait by Z. E. Talbert
Eric Beggs, Photographer
State Preservation Board, Austin, TX

Daniel J. Moody, Jr.

*. . . None of us lay claim or makes boast of genius.
Our hope for success and for promotion of our
purposes of government to protect the safety,
happiness and the prosperity of the people, lies
in the practice of integrity and the simple virtues.
We should have but one guide to direct our course,
and that is the public interest.*

Daniel J. Moody, Jr.
1927

DANIEL J. MOODY, JR.

During the late twenties, prosperity was felt throughout the state. There was rapid growth in industry. Better and longer major highways were built. Attaining wealth was every Texan's goal.

Politically, Ma Ferguson was in trouble. She had abused the pardoning policy. She pardoned two thousand prisoners in a twelve month period. Liberalism and favoritism in the Highway Department also continued to poison her administration. Gossip and discontent were rampant.

A Ferguson had been running for governor for the past twelve years. Some Texans were getting tired of a Ferguson in the State Capitol. Dan "the Man" Moody, who had been attorney general under Miriam Ferguson ran against her. He won by a large majority.

The youngest man to be elevated to such a high post, Dan Moody, fell virtually unchallenged into the job. A tall, redheaded, boyish looking man of thirty-three, he never sought the governor's seat. He was content to be attorney general for two terms until he found himself the chief antagonist against the Fergusons. Several highway contracts were cancelled as a result of lawsuits brought by Moody against the Fergusons.

This controversy with the Ferguson administration forced Daniel Moody into the political gubernatorial arena. He fell into the political ring almost as suddenly as the stock market crashed.

Born June 1, 1893, in Taylor, Dan was the son of the town's first mayor. He attended school in Taylor and entered the University of Texas in 1910.

After a short stint in the military during the war, Dan passed the bar, returned to Taylor, and ran for county attorney. While campaigning for himself, he also campaigned for Pat Neff for governor. When Neff became governor, he appointed Moody to district attorney.

As district attorney, young Moody gained fame by prosecuting and winning a highly publicized case, over the Klan's treatment of a man from Burleson. The *New York Times* reported: "Dan Moody made midnight whipping parties go out of style in his neighborhood."

While governor, Moody carried on his efforts to curb the acts of violence committed by the Klan. He also advocated changes in the constitution. One change would permit the legislature to enact laws regarding civil service. He wanted to assure civil service employees of their continuous job regardless of changing administrations. He also raised the number of supreme court justices from three to nine.

Moody wanted to reorganize the state government, giving the governor power to appoint the important executive officers, who had, heretofore, been elected. He felt these officers should not be independent of the governor or any other executive supervision. He was not successful in this effort.

During Governor Moody's administration, prison problems continued. In four years, the prison population increased by 4,500, and the system lost money. He announced to the legislature that two million dollars was needed to reduce the debt, and set the prison system on a cash basis. The voters, by constitutional amendment, authorized the legislature to set up any method of prison control that seemed wise.

Moody was an industrial man. He favored industry over farming and proposed that both should operate in a centralized system. He was most proud of his reformation of the audit system, which led to regular audits of all departments in the state government.

Midway into Moody's second term as governor, the

Great Depression hit. The postwar prosperity, that had pushed profits and other economic growth indicators higher than in any other previous time in the United States, came to an abrupt end. On October 24, 1929, America woke up to the worst financial disaster in its history. Black Thursday was a day to be remembered.

Soon hundreds of businesses closed. Farmers could no longer sell their produce to processors and many lost their land. Tenant farmers were laid off, and in less than a year, Texas was afflicted with a financial sickness.

The Depression proved a personal disaster for many people, including the governor. Moody did not know how to handle failing banks, nor poverty in the farmlands. In addition, Moody did not know what to do about the boxcars of indigent, young vagabonds that were coming to Texas to search for work. Moody, young and idealistic, floundered. It was too much for one man.

Moody did not seek a third term. He returned to his law practice. In 1942, Moody attempted to unseat Senator W. Lee O'Daniel, but came in a poor third. He continued in politics as chairman of the Democratic State Convention for many years.

Daniel Moody died, May 22, 1966, in Austin at the age of seventy-three.

TEXAS TRIVIA AND TRUTH

Two Rio Grande Valley nurserymen developed the Ruby-red grapefruit.

Ross Shaw Sterling

I think the most important function of this government is to build Texas. Build it industrially, economically, physically, mentally, socially and spiritually. If we cease building, we suffer and die; if we continue, we have prosperity, and prosperity means business. Happiness is the ultimate goal of all and the only true happiness lies in development — progress.

Ross Shaw Sterling
1930

ROSS SHAW STERLING

JANUARY 20, 1931 TO JANUARY 17, 1933

In Texas, it was the best of times and the worst of times. The Great Depression had crippled the economy. Personal and corporate financial holdings had all but vanished. Millionaires were brought down, and lowly tenant farmers were without jobs.

On the other hand, oil was bubbling out of the ground at record rates, and the largest oil well of them all had yet to be discovered. Over production reduced oil income. Prices went from a dollar a barrel to ten cents a barrel. The automobile had arrived in Texas. Fords and Chevys were selling for less than $600 each.

Governor Moody appointed three men to head the new Highway Commission that the Ferguson regime had despoiled with corrupt contracts. Among Moody's appointees was, Houston oil mogul, Ross Sterling.

Ross Sterling was a native of Anahuac, Texas. Born February 11, 1875, he was the eighth of twelve children. His father was from Mississippi, but came to homestead in Texas after the Confederate War. Young Sterling, like most of the boys in Texas at that time, tilled the soil.

At twenty-one he decided business was more to his liking than farming. He began his business career as a merchant and a banker. He opened a feed store in Sour Lake that sold supplies to the oil field operators. He later started a bank in Houston.

Blessed with the Midas touch, every business endeavor Sterling initiated prospered. In Humble, Texas, he created an oil company with the purchase of two wells.

One of the wells was a gusher, and the Humble Oil Company was a success.

From this highly successful oil business, Sterling diversified and entered railway building, management banking, and real estate developing. He founded the *Houston Dispatch* that later merged with the *Houston Post*. By the time he was appointed to the Highway Commission, he was legendary in Texas.

Because Texas had been more than good to him, it was not difficult to persuade Sterling to run for governor. Miriam Ferguson was running again, but Sterling won in the primary by a clear majority.

Sterling felt that Texas must enter the "automobile age." Texas needed roads and major highways to link the state to the national transportation system. Other states were spending increasing amounts on roads, and Texas had to keep pace. The Texas government asked motorists to pay a hefty gasoline tax in order to produce the income for construction and maintenance of a highway system that would be longer and better than any in the United States.

A drought, coupled with the Depression, forced Sterling to call a special session of the legislature. He proposed to cut cotton acreage in the state by 50 percent. The bill was passed, but later declared unconstitutional, so it was never put into effect.

Sterling placed four counties under martial law to temporarily shut down oil production because the government was not regulating distribution in East Texas. The courts later ruled that this act exceeded the authority of the governor.

Sterling's administration was fraught with controversy. One crisis followed another. Because of the Depression, people were unable to pay taxes. Government expenditures were high. Sterling recalled the legislature four different times to help deal with the situation. Times were tough.

Thwarted on every turn, Sterling, nevertheless, ran

for reelection. Previously the public understood that governors were entitled to two terms, but Sterling would not be elected to a second term. Ma Ferguson was again on the Democratic ticket, and she won the primary nomination.

Ross Sterling came to Austin and to the governorship a wealthy and prosperous man. He left broke. He lost his fortune due to the Depression and lack of attention to his business while governor. After his term, he returned to Houston to start over.

Doing what he did best, Sterling amassed another fortune in the oil business. He became president of the Sterling Oil and Refining Company, the American Maid Flour Mills, and the Ross Sterling Investment Company. His reputation reestablished, he served on the board of directors of many major companies in both the public and private sector. Sterling received many honors for his philanthropic work.

He married Maud Abbie Gage in 1898, and together they had five children. Sterling died in Fort Worth on March 25, 1949. He was buried in Houston.

TEXAS TRIVIA AND TRUTH

Each color in the United States and Texas flag is symbolic: red for courage, white for purity and liberty, and blue for loyalty.

James V. Allred

*The day of the political trickster, the day of
"closed-door" logrolling, the day of patronage
trading, the day of political sniping, the day of
political sabotage — these days, all of them,
should pass out with the fogs of yesteryear.
The sunshine of truth should come through
open doors so all may see just how this government is carried on.*

James V. Allred
1935

JAMES V. ALLRED

JANUARY 15, 1935 TO JANUARY 17, 1939

As the Depression continued, it became apparent that relief was mandatory. President Franklin Roosevelt's New Deal relief program was beginning to take shape. A Texas Planning Board was established for a period of four years to set up a "planned recovery for Texas."

Miriam Ferguson's second administration was riddled with conflict. The legislature distrusted her and her husband. Consequently, positive legislation was not forthcoming, and Mrs. Ferguson did not seek reelection. For the first time in twenty years, Texas voters were not confronted by a Ferguson on the ballot. This paved the way for other Democratic hopefuls.

James V. Allred, the attorney general at the time, was prime for the post. Born in Bowie, Texas, on March 29, 1899, "Jimmie" Allred graduated from high school and enrolled in Rice University. Lack of financial support caused him to withdraw before graduation. He served with the United States Immigration Service until he enlisted in the United States Navy during World War I.

Soon after the war, Allred began studying law as a clerk in a Wichita Falls law firm. He received his law degree by correspondence from Cumberland University in Tennessee, and he set up a practice in Wichita Falls.

Considered by many as Texas' last liberal governor, Allred's campaign platform was more middle of the road. He proposed a state commission to regulate public utility rates and practices. He insisted upon the regulation of lobbyists and was highly opposed to any income tax on the already overburdened lower-income citizen. Allred

43

quickly gained a plurality in the primary and easily won the election.

Allred's first term as governor was spent cleaning up after the two Fergusons. Due to the abusive handling of the pardon privilege by "Ma" Ferguson, he believed that an independent board to govern pardons was necessary. Allred also set regulations against chain store monopolies. He increased support for education.

In his second term, Jimmy Allred continued his progressive measures. He instituted a teacher's retirement program. He called for a study to establish a state pension fund for poor Texans. Meanwhile, Roosevelt was passing the Social Security Act.

Three factors stand out as major issues during Allred's term as governor. Jimmie had aligned himself with President Roosevelt and the president's recovery policies. Together, with five strong Texas congressmen, Allred was instrumental in gaining governmental aid for relief. The Federal Emergency Relief Administration provided fifty million dollars in aid that centered around the creation of jobs. Soon, 100,000 men were employed by the CCC (Civilian Conservation Corps), and 600,000 Texans worked for the WPA (Work Projects Administration). During that time, new dams, bridges, stadiums, and roads were built.

As a result of Allred's friendship with the president, Roosevelt was a frequent visitor to Texas. On one visit during a fishing trip, Jimmie introduced the president to Lyndon B. Johnson. Johnson was so taken with the president that he flew back to Washington with him and began working for him.

While in office, Jimmie Allred became known as "The Centennial Governor." He passed legislation to create the Texas Centennial celebration, which marked a century of independence from Mexico. Designed in similar format to the Chicago Worlds Fair, the Centennial was built in Dallas on what is now the grounds of the State Fair of Texas. Governor Allred opened the fair on the first day with a $50,000 jeweled key. The next week President Roosevelt visited the fair.

Governor Allred served two successful terms. When his second term had ended, President Roosevelt appointed him to a district judge position. He remained in this position until 1942 when he resigned to run for the United States Senate. He was defeated by W. Lee O'Daniel, and President Harry Truman reappointed him to the bench.

In 1959, Judge Allred invited a hundred of his friends to lunch at the Driskill Hotel in Austin. "The black-haired, fast-talking Allred was in rare form," a Texas journalist wrote in the *Dallas Morning News.* He introduced every guest by name recalling personal accounts of their friendship. A week later, Allred died unexpectedly while visiting Corpus Christi.

Jimmie Allred married Joe Betsy Miller in Wichita Falls in 1927. The couple had three sons. The former governor was buried in his hometown.

TEXAS TRIVIA AND TRUTH

At the 1932 Olympics in Los Angeles, Texan Mildred "Babe" Didrickson won a silver medal in high jump and a gold medal in both the 80-meter hurdles and the javelin.

Wilbur Lee O'Daniel

Texas is rich in soil, climate and natural resources. Those things are the gift of God. The touch of man is necessary to develop these great gifts. After we have untangled some of our legislative mistakes of the past and placed our government on a sound, constructive, economic business basis, so that the pangs of hunger and poverty of our helpless citizens are appeased, and the minds of our businessmen eased, we shall be ready to enter a new era of industrial and agricultural development which should bring to every man, woman and child in Texas, happiness and prosperity.

Wilbur Lee O'Daniel
1939

W. LEE O'DANIEL

JANUARY 17, 1939 TO AUGUST 4, 1941

By 1938 President Roosevelt's New Deal was coming under attack. Texan and Democrat John Nance Garner was vice-president at the time, so out of party loyalty, the Democrats held firm. Nevertheless discontent with the government was widespread.

However, it was clear that the Depression had given the people a new perspective of the United States government. The federal government was more involved in state affairs than it had ever been. When Roosevelt failed to enlarge the Supreme Court with six additional judges in order to have more support for his welfare programs, Texas businessmen were outraged. The president then shifted his interest to reconstructing the New Deal. He emphasized federal regulation and assistance for the banking industry, through the Federal Deposit Insurance Corporation, which guaranteed deposits in member banks. The federal government then closed weak banks and certified strong banks to reopen. Business resented such large scale intervention by the government when recovery was on its way, and businesses were beginning to prosper.

Though the times were turbulent in national politics, it was a comical time in Texas politics. A well-known radio announcer, flour salesman, and self-proclaimed actor with no political experience decided to run for governor.

A newcomer to Texas, Wilbur Lee O'Daniel, a native of Ohio, had spent most of his adult life in Kansas. He moved to Fort Worth in 1925. As the sales manager for the Burrus Mill and Elevator Company, O'Daniel sponsored a daily radio show and featured four unemployed musicians called the Lightcrust Doughboys. Soon O'Daniel added a few homespun remarks to the lively, hillbilly music. The show was an immediate hit. Texans tuned in every day.

In 1935 O'Daniel bought his own company and began selling Hillbilly Flour. The band became known as the Hillbilly Boys. By now, around a million people were listening to their program.

One day, O'Daniel announced that several people had encouraged him to run for governor. On Palm Sunday, he asked his listeners to send him a penny postcard if they thought he should become a candidate. Fifty thousand responses came. The gubernatorial race of 1938 is remembered as one of the most colorful in Texas history.

Uniting politics with showmanship, O'Daniel followed the format of his radio show. Lively hillbilly music was interspersed with comments and informal philosophy.

O'Daniel's famous slogan was "Less Johnson grass and politicians and more smokestacks and businessmen." His platform rested on an evangelical note supporting the Ten Commandments and thirty dollars a month pension for everyone over sixty-five years old.

Few politicians took O'Daniel's candidacy seriously. Newspaper editors ridiculed the possibility of electing the yodeling, flour salesman. Businessmen discounted the probability of O'Daniel surviving the primary.

But the man who had taken up the slogan "Please pass the biscuits, Pappy" from his radio show, fooled them all. O'Daniel bought a bus, and with his family and band, toured the state. The fact that he could not vote himself, as he had failed to pay his poll tax, was meaningless to the voters. Pappy Lee O'Daniel beat twelve other competitors without a runoff.

Personality and showmanship were now in politics. Name identification was the key and public involvement was the style. The new governor was inaugurated in the University of Texas football stadium with children attending and bands playing. When the governor's daughter married, he announced it on his Sunday morning radio program and invited the public to attend. Some 25,000 people came to Austin for the affair. With the help of a loud speaker system set up on the grounds of the Governor's Mansion, everyone was included.

Governor O'Daniel could not possibly fulfill his campaign promise. There was not enough money in the state treasury to pay thirty dollars per person, per month to everyone over sixty-five. Even though the economy was recovering, he had difficulty passing legislation. Some people considered O'Daniel a lame duck from the moment he took office.

Governor O'Daniel ran again in 1941 against Mrs. Ferguson and won. Before his second term was over, he resigned to run for the United States Senate. His opponent was Jimmie Allred. He won this race, as well.

Other government officials considered Pappy Lee O'Daniel an ignorant, ineffective showman. But the public loved him. When his term in the Senate was over, he moved back to Dallas to establish an insurance company. He ran for governor two more times, but was defeated each time. His popularity had run its course.

O'Daniel died in Dallas on May 11, 1969.

TEXAS TRIVIA AND TRUTH

The New London School in New London, Texas, exploded March 18, 1937, killing 293 people.

Coke R. Stevenson

The problems of tomorrow will be different, but demands for faith in our ability to meet them remain the same. The Brazos River men knew their task was enormous, but they faced it cheerfully. Theirs was a task of conquering raw land, but they had no necessity for concern about the dignity of the individual. That dignity had been established by their forefathers for generations, and no force of regimentation had come forward to challenge it. Our task of producing from the land is not less than theirs, but we have the added responsibility of maintaining the dignity and self-respect of the individual.

Coke R. Stevenson
1945

COKE R. STEVENSON

Almost anyone would have made a better governor than W. Lee O'Daniel. Roosevelt was still in the White House, and Texans were more Democratic than ever. They blamed the hard times on the Hoover administration. They also believed that Roosevelt was responsible for the economic recovery. Most Texans thought the economic prosperity they were experiencing was a result of World War II. Before the war, Texas had not been highly industrialized. Now defense plants dotted the countryside from Texarkansas to El Paso.

When W. Lee O'Daniel resigned his post as governor to take a seat in the United States Senate, Lieutenant Governor Coke Stevenson assumed his position. Texans were so involved with the war and international affairs that the ascension of Stevenson as governor was almost unnoticed. Stevenson entered state government in 1928 as a representative, served two terms as Speaker of the House, and two terms as lieutenant governor. Coke R. Stevenson, named for a former governor, Richard Coke, slipped easily into the role of governor.

Coke Stevenson was born in a log cabin in Mason County on March 20, 1888. He grew up in Junction in Kimble County. He had little schooling, but studied history and bookkeeping on his own. He also took correspondence courses. Before he turned twenty years old, he had worked in his father's mercantile store, and started a freight business, driving wagons between Junction and Brady. Later he became a janitor for the Junction State Bank and soon became a cashier. He studied law at night and passed the bar in 1913.

51

Coke, always industrious and hard working, started the First National Bank in Junction. He also became involved in other business establishments, such as a movie theater, a warehouse company, an automobile agency, a weekly newspaper, a pharmaceutical business, and a hotel.

A tall, pipe-smoking westerner, somewhat resembling the Marlboro Man, Coke was enterprising and tireless. As a young man, he built his own home out of salvaged lumber.

As governor, he was a far cry from the colorful Pappy O'Daniel. Often called "Calculating Coke," the contrast in personality was welcomed. Coke was quiet, shrewd, dignified, and cautious. He was the first governor who claimed the dubious title of "workaholic."

Serving during wartime, Governor Stevenson went about his job with one thing in mind — to help America win the war. For him, state government became secondary to national considerations.

Texans, for the second time in that century, were called to serve their country. Those who stayed at home endured wartime rationing, wage and price controls, blackouts, and air raid drills. They faithfully bought war bonds, took Red Cross training, and grew victory gardens. Many worked in the oil industry that supplied the oil for the ships, trucks, tanks, and planes that moved against the enemy. Due to federal contracts, the rate of industrial activity in Texas rose to an all-time high.

Governor Stevenson was a strong believer in fiscal responsibility and prohibited the legislature from spending more money than it took in. He started the pay-as-you-go plan. His administration, that started with a deficit in the treasury, ended with a surplus. During Stevenson's administration, the "Good Roads" amendment passed, which allowed the state to dedicate tax revenue to building and maintaining roads. This helped produce one of the nation's best and most extensive highway systems.

To his credit, Stevenson liked to maintain a good relationship with Mexico, and during his tenure, managed to persuade the Texas legislature to pass a bill giving Mexican immigrants all the rights and privileges of Texas citizens.

"Mr. Texas," as many later called him, was seldom seen without his favorite pipe. Many times he used it as a gavel while presiding over the House. He told everyone that he hated politics but loved government. "Less government is the best government" was his motto, and accordingly, he believed Texas could prosper if left alone to its own hard work and thrift.

Governor Stevenson seldom spoke out against controversial issues. He kept his own counsel and repeated his own Beatitude often: Blessed is he who sayeth nothing, for he shall not be misquoted.

Coke Stevenson served as governor more consecutive years than anyone previously. After five and a half years, he turned the job over to his successor and sought a seat in the United States Senate. He lost, in a highly controversial race, to Lyndon Baines Johnson. Johnson campaigned in his own helicopter called the "Johnson City Windmill." It was the closest Senate race ever. Johnson won by only eighty-seven votes.

Finished with politics, Stevenson returned to his beloved ranch in Junction. He died on June 28, 1975, at the age of eighty-seven.

TEXAS TRIVIA AND TRUTH

The longest distance across Texas in a straight line is 801 miles.

Beauford Halbert Jester

Government should face up to and endeavor to alleviate the sins of modern society which Canon Frederick Lewis Donaldson, of Westminister Abbey, enumerates as "policies without principles, wealth without work, pleasure without conscience, knowledge without character, industry without morality, science without humanity, worship (and I shall add, public service) without sacrifice."

In all areas of governmental activity we must choose the high road and the middle path between extremes.

Beauford Halbert Jester
1949

BEAUFORD H. JESTER

JANUARY 21, 1947–JULY 11, 1949

America was finally at peace. On December 31, 1946, President Harry Truman, who had assumed the presidency when President Roosevelt died, formally ended World War II. He further ended all wage, price and salary controls, thus eliminating wartime rations. The classic film "The Best Years of Our Lives" came out and the country, feeling good about itself, was preparing to stabilize the economy. Texas was doing the same.

On the political front, the fractions were flying. Lyndon Johnson had won a bitterly fought Senate race against former governor Coke Stevenson. "Landslide Lyndon" weathered accusations of fraud and election irregularities and retained his seat in the Senate.

The gubernatorial race, pale by comparison, was not without spice of derision. Beauford Jester ran against the former president of the University of Texas, Homer Rainey. The controversy arose over a book, John Dos Passos', *U.S.A.,* and though Jester won, the Democratic party was beginning to splinter.

Beauford Halbert Jester was born, January 12, 1893, in Corsicana, Texas. From a prominent family, Jester went to the University of Texas where he became known as the "big man on campus." From there, he proceeded to attend Harvard. When World War I began, he left Harvard and joined the army. After attending officers training school, he was commissioned an officer and eventually served in Germany as a captain in the 90th Division. After the war, he returned to the University of Texas and received his law degree.

This wavy-haired, smooth-talking young man accumulated a great deal of wealth as an oil industry attorney and railroad commissioner. Politically astute, Jester followed the "peoples path" philosophy, which served him well during his gubernatorial campaign. Outgoing and amiable, he loved people and enjoyed campaigning in small towns never visited by other candidates.

Soon after Jester's inauguration, Texas experienced an unprecedented disaster. On April 16, 1949, a ship, sitting in the harbor at Texas City, blew up. It was loaded with explosive nitrate. Over 550 people were killed, and hundreds were injured. Governor Jester immediately supplied over $35 million for relief and recovery.

Jester was a popular governor. Cheerful and open to all his constituents, he was able to make giant strides in the postwar era. His first successful attempt to implement change occurred when he convinced the legislature to increase appropriations without new taxes. Hospitals and orphanages received a shot in the arm with new revenues. Also a controversial labor law passed, making it illegal to require an employee to join a labor union.

The most remembered bill that passed during Jester's administration was the Gilmer-Aiken program modernizing the state school system. One of the most debated issues to ever pass the legislature, the bill redirected and revitalized all Texas schools. Not only did it provide for the reorganization of the entire school system from the local to the state level, the bill also created an elective State Board of Education. A "Minimum Foundation Program," which assured every child nine months of quality schooling for twelve years, was included. The bill further stipulated that the system would be automatically funded, and the legislature would not have to vote on it every two years. The Gilmer-Aiken Bill doubled the state's spending for public education overnight.

This bill caused legislators to stay in session longer than any previous time in Texas history. The session lasted from January 11, 1949, until July 6, 1949. Afterwards, the legislature set a time limit on the sessions to 140 days.

During Jester's administration, the repeal of the poll tax legislation occurred. This was a landmark decision. Governor Jester signed the act which stated that all Texans, no matter if they paid a poll tax or owned property, could now vote in any election.

Beauford Jester's political career was unfortunately cut short. On July 11, 1949, Governor Jester was riding an overnight train going to Galveston to make a speech. When the porter attempted to wake him up the next morning, he found the governor dead. Beauford Jester had died of a heart attack.

Known as a polished politician who enjoyed the company of many friends and supporters, Jester's fine record suggests he could have served Texas for many years. Though some might have considered him a "playboy," others said that Jester was one of the most effective governors Texas ever had.

TEXAS TRIVIA AND TRUTH

Admiral Chester A. Nimitz, a native Texan and a five star admiral, accepted the surrender of the Japanese ending World War II in the Pacific on September 2, 1945.

Allan Shivers

As we stand here today and try to look ahead, there are clouds on the horizon whose somber hue is unmistakable. Before the wreckage of one vast conflict has been cleared way, the world is threatened with another war more terrible than the last. The godless flag of Communism unfurling its dishonest hate, greed and lust would consume a free people.

We have all hoped and prayed that some near-miracle of international diplomacy, or some real miracle of brotherly love, will yet save us from World War III.

Allan Shivers
1951

ALLAN SHIVERS

JULY 16, 1949 TO JANUARY 15, 1957

In the early fifties federal funds continued to flow into Texas by way of defense contracts. Industry was surpassing agriculture. Cities like Houston and Dallas were gaining sophistication and growing rapidly. They were achieving a high-profile status similar to the larger cities of the East like New York, Chicago, and Philadelphia.

Over the political scene, two ominous clouds were hovering. Fearful that the Communists were going to take over the country, a near panic arose when Sen. Joseph McCarthy began his public investigation of politicians and private citizens alike. McCarthy accused them of being either Communist sympathizers or members of the Communist party. Red mania was rampant.

Citizens were becoming disenchanted with President Truman, due to his civil rights position and the escalation of the Korean War. The Democratic party's image and policies were coming into question.

In Texas, political fervor was pale by comparison. Governor Jester had died unexpectedly on a train to Galveston. Allan Shivers, the lieutenant governor, was sworn in on July 12, 1948, with little fanfare. The state government was to proceed as if nothing had changed; it was business as usual.

Allan Shivers was born October 5, 1907, in Lufkin, Texas. He grew up in Woodville, where his father was county judge. His family moved to Port Arthur when he was a teenager, and Allen finished high school there. Afterwards, he enrolled in the University of Texas. He paid his way by working in the Texas Company refinery and by selling shoes. He became president of the student body and passed the bar exam before he graduated from law school. A short four years later, he unseated the state senator from Jefferson County and was dubbed the "boy senator."

Allan entered the service when World War II broke out. He achieved the rank of major and served overseas as an intelligence officer.

Shivers, tall, dark and often wearing a Stetson hat, looked like a stand-in for John Wayne. Six feet two inches tall, his presence alone commanded attention. Occasionally, he attracted suspicion and ridicule by wearing pearl-grey spats (cloth covering the tops of his shoes and his ankles) and sporting an expensive walking cane. This wardrobe came after he had secured his financial future by marrying a multimillionaire's daughter, Marialice Shary.

At forty-one, Allan Shivers was prepared for the role of governor. He was a born leader. After his initial, successful run for the Senate, he never lost an election. Elected as lieutenant governor under Jester, Shivers was preparing to run for governor when Jester retired, but fate sped up the process.

Governor Shivers served Texas longer than any other governor to this date, which speaks admirably of his political durability. Although reputed as a conservative Democrat, Governor Shivers' accomplishments were more liberal than conservative. During his tenure, the "Shivercrats," as they were known, turned from their party loyalty and supported Gen. Dwight D. Eisenhower, a Republican, for president. This infuriated the conservative Democrats. Eisenhower favored state control of offshore oil, and Shivers concurred. He believed offshore oil regulation was in Texas' best interest, because of the state's long and potentially productive coastline.

Integration versus segregation was becoming a hot issue. Shivers was critical of the Supreme Court's decision outlawing segregation in public schools. He encouraged local school districts to integrate without federal pressure. By 1955, eighty-four Texas school districts had voluntarily integrated. This small step toward desegregation was more progress than all other southern states combined.

After fulfilling the term vacated by the death of Jester, Shivers managed to serve three consecutive terms. Liberal Ralph Yarborough bitterly contested Shivers' last race. Nevertheless, Shivers won by a scant margin.

The debate over the rights of offshore oil production continued, undercutting and diminishing Shivers' political base. Shivers realized his power was rapidly eroding.

Liberals and loyalists, controlled the Democratic State Convention. When Shivers again refused to support the Democratic nominee, the die was cast. A coalition, led by Rep. Sam Rayburn and Sen. Lyndon Johnson, ousted Shivers as party leader. Shivers' political career was over.

To his credit, Governor Shivers had substantial achievements during his long tenure. He increased appropriations for state hospitals, and he levied a tax on natural gasoline to cover the increasing expense of state government. He passed a law creating the Commission of Education, which, ideally, would unify and coordinate services and curriculum for the state colleges and universities.

After his three terms as governor, Allan Shivers retired to Mission, Texas, to pursue his many business interests. He died January 14, 1985.

TEXAS TRIVIA AND TRUTH

The first leg of the Gulf Freeway connecting Houston and Galveston was dedicated August 14, 1952.

Portrait by Victor Lallier
Eric Beggs, Photographer
State Preservation Board, Austin, TX

Price Daniel

Texas today has over 175 separate departments, agencies, and boards . . . we have 213 separate funds in the State Treasury and over thirty separate funds deposited in banks without ever entering the Treasury . . . so it shall be the aim of this administration not only to balance the budget this year and provide for the needs of the next biennium, but also to maintain the pay-as-you-go program intended by our Constitution and lay the ground work for a permanent and more efficient reorganization of state government.

Price Daniel
1959

PRICE DANIEL

A lead story in the November 23, 1956, issue of *U.S. News and World Report* claimed "Texas, an empire within a republic, is shaping up as the new powerhouse of the United States. In the Lone Star State, oil fields are booming. Big, new industries are springing up. Quiet towns are being transformed, almost violently, into large cities with towering skylines."

The Texas economy outgrew the rest of the states in the production of oil, petrochemicals, natural gas, black carbon, helium, sulfur, and cotton — to name only a few. Agriculture was boasting a 56 percent increase over the previous six years. Texas was also growing in population. Ten of the nation's fastest growing cities were within Texas' borders. Optimistic, Governor Shivers proclaimed as he left office, "I think the growth of Texas is unlimited."

Conservative Democrats called upon Price Daniel to run for governor to continue their stand on segregation.

Marion Price Daniel was born October 10, 1910, in Dayton, Texas. After graduating from high school in Fort Worth and working for a short time for the *Fort Worth Star-Telegram,* he entered Baylor University. At Baylor, he studied journalism and law. He received his law degree in 1932, and he was almost immediately admitted to the bar.

In six short years, Daniel was elected to the Texas House of Representatives as a moderate, New Deal Democrat. Like most legislators at the time, Daniel stepped aside and helped the United States in battle. He served in the army from 1943 to 1946, starting as a private and ending his military career as a captain.

As soon as he was discharged from the service, Daniel was elected attorney general without opposition. By the time he was elected governor, he could say at his inauguration that he had taken an official oath of public service nine times — three times as a member of the legislature, once as Speaker of the House, once as a serviceman, three times as attorney general of Texas, and once as a member of the United States Senate. No man was better qualified for the governor's seat.

Governor Daniel first made this mark while he was attorney general. He fought for the tidelands of Texas. While he was senator, he introduced the Tidelands Bill, which President Eisenhower signed, giving Texas rights to its offshore oil.

The civil rights issue was heating up. Governor Daniel's position was "interposition," which was a doctrine by which states were allowed to execute their own policies, regardless of what the federal government stipulated. Governor Daniel was thwarted on this front. The civil rights issue was shaking the foundation of the Democratic party's political control in Texas.

Internally, the governor was ferreting out the cause of many scandals, which included insurance companies that were abusing their authority, and lobbyist accused of malfeasance for giving elaborate gifts as bribes to legislators.

The governor was also knee-deep in the issue over a state sales tax. Some believed that a state sales tax was the only fair tax since everyone paid according to their purchases. Daniel disliked it. Nevertheless, the bill passed without the governor's signature. At first, it was a modest two percent tax. Under Governor Connally the sales tax increased to four percent and continued upward through the next five governors. Fortunately, both liberals and conservatives agreed that the sales tax had provided the state with enough revenue to make substantial advancements, and allowed the state to operate without a deficit.

Three Texans were attracting national attention:

Ralph Yarborough, Lyndon Johnson, and John Connally. Ralph Yarborough continued to run for governor every two years as a liberal Democrat. Lyndon Johnson was seeking the presidency, and Texans were shouting, "All the way with LBJ." John Connally was considering abandoning his Washington post in order to solidify the Democrats in Texas by running for governor of Texas.

Governor Daniel tried for a fourth term, but the popular, silver-tongued John Connally defeated him. Daniel retired from state government after twenty-four years of service. He later served the federal government as assistant to the president for federal-state relations and director of the Office of Emergency Preparedness. He was appointed to the Texas Supreme Court in 1971 and served until his retirement in 1979.

Price Daniel is married to Jean Houston Baldwin, the great-great-granddaughter of Sam Houston and great-granddaughter of former Gov. Tom Campbell. Their son, Price Daniel, Jr., was at one time Speaker of the House and chairman of the 1974 Constitutional Convention. Daniel retired to his home in Lubbock, where he still resides.

TEXAS TRIVIA AND TRUTH

Harris County was chosen as the site for the National Aeronautics and Space Administration's manned spacecraft center, and NASA was born.

John Bowden Connally

In our age of growing complexity, surely man is entitled to other compelling freedoms: Freedom to dream. Freedom to venture. Freedom to work. Freedom to think. Freedom to be an individual.

A man should have the freedom to seek great riches. He should have the freedom to espouse great teachings. He should have the freedom from group opposition. And he should have the freedom to live in modest means with tranquility and serenity, if that be his choice. He should not be reduced to a common denominator, to an average. For the truth is, there is no average of ambition, no average of determination, no average of faith.

John Bowden Connally
1967

JOHN BOWDEN CONNALLY

JANUARY 15, 1963 TO JANUARY 21, 1969

Lone Star statesmen had made major contributions
to the nation's political process, but only as consultants,
never as chief executives. Lyndon Johnson's failure to
attain the Democratic nomination indicated a national
disenchantment with Texans. And John F. Kennedy, the
dashing, charismatic young leader, easily made it to the
White House despite his Catholic religion. Lyndon
Johnson, who lost the nomination, was reluctantly
tapped by Kennedy to be vice-president. The party
needed Johnson's support to carry Texas. Otherwise,
Johnson was considered a political liability.

While in Texas, feuding among Democrats was rising to the danger point. The two factions, the liberals and
the conservatives, were at each others' throats. Texas
was in serious danger of losing its strong Democratic col-
umn in the electoral college. In order to help heal the
party's weakening position, Johnson persuaded Kennedy
to make a trip to Texas. History took an unusual turn at
the underpass in Dallas.

The tragic event on November 22, 1963, was of international proportions. President Kennedy and Governor
Connally were shot during a motorcade in Dallas. The
shots killed Kennedy, and seriously wounded Connally.
Suddenly a Texan named Lyndon Baines Johnson became president of the United States. Despite the circumstances, John Connally was pleased that his longtime
friend had finally become president.

John Connally, often called "Big John" because of his
physical height and his political stature, was a Texan
through and through. Born in Floresville, Texas, on Feb-

ruary 27, 1917, he was the son of Lela and John Bowden Connally, a tenant farmer. He attended public schools in San Antonio and Floresville, then entered the University of Texas, where he received his law degree in 1941.

Connally joined the Naval Reserve immediately upon graduation. He worked in the office of the chief of naval operations and later on the planning staff of General Eisenhower. He also served as a fighter plane director aboard the aircraft carrier USS *Essex* in the Pacific. He was awarded the Bronze Star, and for his service aboard the aircraft carrier USS *Bennington,* the Legion of Merit. He completed his active military career as a lieutenant commander, but he remained in the Naval Reserve until 1954.

Connally was appointed Secretary of the Navy in 1960 by President Kennedy. After Kennedy's tragic death and Connally's recovery, Connally returned to Texas to run for governor. His name identification served him well, and he was elected to three consecutive terms.

As governor of Texas, Connally almost single-handedly preserved the one-party system despite the constant political badgering by the more sophisticated and well-financed Republican organization.

All legislation was labeled "Connallization" as Big John perpetually had his hand in the process. The economy experienced modest gains during Connally's tenure. He was a big promoter of Texas tourism, and during his last year, the state enjoyed more than twenty million tourists who spent over one billion dollars within the state's borders. In 1968 Connally boasted that 1,494 new industrial plants had moved to Texas, and more than 1,976 plants had expanded, creating 150,000 new jobs. Even though he was a conservative, he passed a law allowing pari-mutuel betting and racetracks as his parting shot from the capital.

In 1970 President Richard Nixon appointed Connally secretary of the treasury, an unheard of move for a Republican president. Connally soon became what James

Reston described in the *New York Times* as "the spunki-est character in Washington these days."

To support Nixon fully in his reelection, Connally surprised the political world by changing parties. After Nixon's election, Connally had hopes of attaining the coveted position of secretary of state. However, the job went to Henry Kissinger.

Connally moved again to Texas, and after a brief and unsuccessful bid for the presidency in 1980, he returned to private business. As a private citizen, he had gained much wealth as attorney and executor of Sid Richardson's estate. During the real estate and bank crisis of the 1980s, Connally, however, lost his entire fortune.

A flamboyant, colorful, larger-than-life Texan, Connally was one of the state's star heroes. He loved the pomp and circumstances of his life as he walked with presidents of nations and heads of billion-dollar corporations. He surrounded himself with trappings of authority. As governor, his bodyguards were always with him, though never taller than him. He insisted that the Rangers who were assigned to him be three inches shorter. He established a legend, then lived the legend to the fullest.

John Connally married Idanell Brill in 1938. They had three children: John III, Sharon, and Mark. Connally died in 1993, and the rich and famous of the nation attended his funeral.

TEXAS TRIVIA AND TRUTH

Ed White of San Antonio made the famous first walk in space on June 3, 1965.

Preston E. Smith

The turbulent seas we sailed throughout the 1960s are quieting. The 1970s once again hold promise, not bewilderment and despair, for the peoples of the greatest nation on earth. This does not mean that we are sailing into safe harbors of the past. The past is closed forever. But, the future open wide before us.

. . . If we are, indeed, entering a new era, it must be a time in which we are totally honest with ourselves. It must be a time in which we are totally honest with the young people for whom the mantle of leadership is waiting. The concept that all growth is automatic progress should be cast out.

. . . Materialism must be rejected in favor of human compassion and dignity. The responsibilities of our State in keeping its air clean, its rivers and lakes clear, and its people healthy must be accepted.

Preston E. Smith
1971

PRESTON E. SMITH

JANUARY 21, 1969 TO JANUARY 16, 1973

While Washington, the nation's capital, was under siege by Americans protesting the war in Vietnam, Texans were ironing out their own discontent. In November of 1969, 250,000 war protestors marched from the Capitol up Pennsylvania Avenue to the Washington Monument. Some carried coffins, while others painted peace symbols on the monument. President Nixon vowed to gradually withdraw the troops from Vietnam. This did not satisfy the angry mob. University students rebelled with violence. The United States was in a war it could not win. In further protest, a National Guardsman fired into a crowd of protestors at Kent State University killing four people.

In Texas, a new problem was brewing. The drug, marijuana, was surfacing on its borders, and quietly permeating into the hands of its young people.

Politically, Texans were making few waves. When John Connally bowed out of Texas politics, Preston Smith was easily elected as the thirty-eighth governor.

No other candidate had so effectively and steadily built his ladder to the top. Smith had served three terms in the Texas House of Representatives from 1945–1951. He served six years in the state Senate from 1957–1963, and had a record of three terms as lieutenant governor from 1963–1969.

With his election, Governor Smith became the first lieutenant governor to be elected governor since 1857, when Hardin R. Runnels defeated Sam Houston.

Preston Smith was born on a farm, in Williamson County, on March 8, 1912. He was the seventh of thirteen children. He attended public school in Williamson and Gaines counties and graduated from high school in Lamesa.

Economic conditions were deplorable in West Texas during Smith's younger days. Drought, dust storms, and the Great Depression left farm families with little money. While attending high school, Smith worked in a grocery store/filling station. When he enrolled in Texas Technological College (now Texas Tech University), he and a friend started their own service station. He earned only twenty dollars a month working seven days a week.

Soon after his marriage to Ima Smith, his high school sweetheart, Smith set up a movie theater in an abandoned laundry building near the college campus. He parlayed this business into six movie houses in Lubbock, Texas.

Preston Smith, the first governor to come from West Texas, had learned the business of state government from the bottom up. His long relationship with the Texas legislature groomed him for the top job. Though not as colorful, nor articulate, as his predecessor, Smith demonstrated that not all politicians had to be six feet tall to be politically astute. Quietly, but effectively, he had cultivated voters throughout the state so that his election was one of the easiest in Texas history.

In many ways Preston Smith was an impressive governor. His accomplishments were numerous. He increased aid for vocational education, established two new medical schools, and reduced the voting age to eighteen. He also improved the state's water supply system — an extremely helpful act in the western portion of the state. The highway signs stating "Drive Friendly" were Smith's idea. They mark every highway in Texas even today.

Lacking the sizzle of a good West Texas steak, Smith used other methods of endearing himself to the public. He wore a polka dot tie to add a dash of color to his demeanor. He also took a "hands-on" approach to the office. He answered his own telephone with, "This is Preston Smith. I am your governor," and he encouraged fellow Texans to come straight to the top. He also invited the press to his door, but wisely shunned television coverage that would expose his ineptness as a public speaker.

As a West Texas farm boy, Governor Smith believed in hard work and the golden rule. He met his fellow Texan one-on-one and did his best work person-to-person. He established an open-door policy and prided himself in being accessible to everyone. As one who always enjoyed a good joke, he never took himself too seriously.

In 1971, almost immediately into Smith's second term, Texans were shaken by the disclosure of the Sharpstown Scandal. The Federal Securities and Exchange Commission accused Speaker of the House Gus Mutscher and two of his aides of participating in a scheme to aid and abet Frank Sharp, a Houston banker, in evading federal scrutiny. Many prominent people were implicated, and a thorough investigation removed Mutscher and his friends from office. Governor Smith, a stockholder in the bank, was vindicated because he had vetoed one of the bills designed to favor Mr. Sharp.

The Sharpstown Scandal hurt Governor Smith politically. It proved to be a major factor in his attempt to win a third term in the governor's office. Smith lost to Dolph Briscoe.

After his defeat, Smith and his family returned to Lubbock, where they now live.

TEXAS TRIVIA AND TRUTH

The total land and inland water area of Texas is 267,339 square miles, and about two hundred species of freshwater fish are found in Texas.

Dolph Briscoe, Jr.

In this state we love under a Texas Bill of Rights.
. . . Each Texan has a right to privacy, free from un-
just harassment or intrusion by government officials or
anyone else. Each Texan has a right to health care
which is effective, readily available and affordable in
all part of the state, urban and rural. Each Texan has a
right to a clean and fruitful environment, including ad-
equate supply of water for every area of the state, and
an adequate supply of energy for the essential needs of
our society. Each Texan has a right to mobility, the
ways and means to transport himself and his goods
from one place to another by highway, rail, water or
air. Each Texan has a right to decent treatment when
he is young, dignity when he is old, and opportunity
throughout his life, regardless of his race or sex. It is to
these rights that I pledge myself and my efforts.

Dolph Briscoe, Jr.
1975

DOLPH BRISCOE, JR.

JANUARY 16, 1973 TO JANUARY 16, 1979

Texas had reluctantly become a two-party state.
Texas politics was becoming more diverse. Not only were
women entering the political arena more than ever, but
African Americans and Hispanics were seeking seats in
the Texas legislature. Barbara Jordan of Houston was
elected to the Texas Senate, and Curtis Graves of Houston was elected to the House. State Legislator Frances
"Sissy" Farenthold, of Corpus Christi, was instrumental
in passing the Open Records Law, requiring state officials to report campaign donations. Texas teetered on the
brink of political change, but the wheels of change continued to move slowly.

Preston Smith's failure to win a third term set the
stage for a relative newcomer, Dolph Briscoe, Jr. Dolph
represented his district in the state legislature from
1949–1957, but few people remembered him. Although
an active Democrat, he sought no other office until he ran
for governor.

Dolph Briscoe, Jr., was born in Uvalde, Texas, on
April 23, 1923, the son of Dolph and Georgie Briscoe. He
graduated from the University of Texas and soon enlisted in the United States Army. As an officer, he served
in the Far East.

After the war, he returned to Uvalde to follow in his
father's footsteps in the ranching business. Dolph Briscoe, Sr., formed a ranching partnership with former Gov.
Ross Sterling in the early twenties. By the time young
Briscoe was ready to take over, the ranch had grown to
over a million acres of southwest Texas land, one of the

largest in the world. Briscoe soon ranked among the richest men in Texas. Young Briscoe had found his life's work and his lifetime home.

Not having to worry about finances, Briscoe went to work for his city and state. He served on almost every civic board in his area with an unblemished reputation and great popularity. Briscoe headed organizations such as the Cattlemen's Association, Sheep and Goat Raiser, and the South Texas Chamber of Commerce. He was a cattle rancher's ideal of a true Texan.

Campaigning for governor, Briscoe took to the sky. In his private plane, he flew across Texas like a crop duster, meeting people on a one-to-one basis. Texans were still politically conservative. They shied from anyone labeled liberal, especially if the liberal was a woman. Frances "Sissy" Farenhold, a state legislator, believed it was time for another woman governor and was campaigning competitively. In the end, Dolph Briscoe won both the Democratic nomination and the general election by a narrow margin.

As governor, Briscoe set out to restore confidence in government which was lost during the scandal-ridden administration of Preston Smith. Often dubbed as a caretaker governor, Briscoe, nonetheless, made his mark in education, road development, and reconstruction of the constitution. Briscoe increased funding for public schools and higher education. He also fulfilled his main objective, the one he started years back while in the legislature — enhancing the farm to market roads system in Texas.

Unlike most governors, Briscoe had the unique privilege of serving the state when it was trouble free. Briscoe's biggest problem was how best to dispose of the surplus in the budget. Oil taxes had escalated revenues to the point that the government had $3 billion over the budget.

During Briscoe's term, many constitutional revisions were made. The main revision was setting the governor's term of office. For the first time in Texas history, the term for governor was changed from two years to four years.

Briscoe easily won his second term. But he lost his third term to a fresh, highly affluent, outspoken Republican, William P. Clements, Jr.

Historians might say that Dolph Briscoe would not have fared well as governor during any other period in Texas' history. Had the times been turbulent, Briscoe, perhaps, would have faltered. He lacked the aggressiveness required for crisis situations. He was often criticized for his absenteeism. He preferred his ranch home to the Governor's Mansion. Others attacked his slowness to act and his inaccessibility, all of which, no doubt, sabotaged his goal to serve the state as governor for ten years.

After his political career, Briscoe, still a young man, returned to Uvalde. Many honors and awards came to him in the subsequent years, and he is still remembered by many as one of the most gentle men to ever serve at the Capitol.

Dolph Briscoe and his wife Betty Jane have three children.

TEXAS TRIVIA AND TRUTH

In July of 1974, Congressman Barbara Jordan of Texas delivered her famous "We the People" speech before the Democratic National Convention.

William P. Clements, Jr.

Texas has reached maturity. We have grown into an integral part of the national economy, and yes, even the international economy, and we must think in those global terms . . . not because we have failed but because we have succeeded and grown.

It is forecast that Texas will be the second in population among the states and our gross economy is now over $300 billion a year. If Texas was still an independent sovereign republic, our Texas economy would be number thirteen in the world.

It is a part of this maturity that we must live, work and compete in a very tough world.

William P. Clements, Jr.
1987

WILLIAM P. CLEMENTS, JR.

JANUARY 16, 1979 TO JANUARY 18, 1983

Texas was fast becoming known as a can-do state. Major advancements were being made in technology. Huge corporations like gophers were springing up from the native soil in West Texas, and prosperity was abounding.

When the 1980 census was taken, the results showed a mosaic of cultures. Ethnic groups were growing and newer role models were emerging.

Politically, Texas was on the verge of a giant moodswing. The Republican party was clearly making it a two-party state. Ronald Reagan was riding a new wave of patriotism into the White House, and William P. Clements, Jr., was riding a white stallion into the Texas Capitol.

William P. Clements, Jr., was the first Republican to serve as governor of Texas in over a hundred years. He served two nonconsecutive terms. During the twelve years of his on-and-off tenure, Texas hit the highs of prosperity and the lows of financial despair. As a businessman, Clements represented the prototype of Texas' volatile story. Much like a Texas tornado, his election came as a surprise attack on the staid Democrats, who believed they had a monopoly on politics in Texas.

William P. Clements, Jr., was born in Dallas, Texas, on April 13, 1917. After graduating from Highland Park High School, Clements went to work as a "roughneck" in the oil fields. Following the hot spots of oil production, young Clements was able to finance his engineering education at Southern Methodist University.

Restless, he withdrew from school after two years, and returned to the oil fields. In 1947, he and two partners borrowed money to buy two drilling rigs. This partnership formed Sedco, a company that became the largest offshore drilling company in the world. In a short twenty years, William "Bill" Clements became one of the wealthiest men in Texas.

In 1973, President Nixon nominated Clements to serve as deputy secretary at the United States Department of Defense. He received the Distinguished Public Service Award.

Deciding to run for governor, Clements was virtually unknown beyond the Republican party. To overcome his lack of name identification, he pledged $7 million to his campaign. He easily won the Republican nomination. To the surprise of the Democrats, Dolph Briscoe, the incumbent, did not receive the Democratic nomination. Attorney General John Hill, a liberal Democrat, won the Democrat's support.

Clements campaigned as a conservative businessman. He promised to reduce state spending, reduce taxes, and streamline the state's heavy bureaucracy. Many believed that the discontent of most Texans with President Jimmy Carter, at the time, gave Clements the edge he needed to win over the popular and well-established John Hill.

During Clement's first term, he cut the state payroll by 5 percent a year and vetoed a record $250 million for the budget. A tough, no nonsense attitude worked well for Clements in the first half of his term, but gradually, his gruff, flippant remarks began to alienate many voters. As a result, a young Democrat, by the name of Mark White, won the Democratic primary.

Faced with healing his arrogant image, Clements raised and spent nearly $12 million on his reelection bid. By this time, the economy in Texas was in serious trouble, and unemployment was at an all-time high. Texans thought that Clements had bungled the job. White won by a surprising margin.

Never to forget a political insult, Clements again entered the race for governor in 1986. This time Texans believed only a businessman could save them from further economic disaster. It was a bitter race with Clements winning. Clements felt vindicated, and the Republicans interpreted the win as an indicator that their ranks were growing in Texas.

With the economy continuing to plummet, Clements hit a thick row of stumps during his second turn as governor. A state budget deficit, approaching $1 billion, loomed ominously in his path. A record unemployment figure followed. Prisons were overcrowded, and Texas was under a federal order to improve them immediately. Against all that Clements stood for, he was forced to endorse a new budget that included new taxes.

In the midst of his economic troubles, a scandal hit the sports world. Clements was chairman of the Board of Trustees for Southern Methodist University when the school was placed on probation for improper recruiting and payment of athletes. Clements was compelled to admit his involvement. The scandal permanently damaged SMU. The football program at the university has not fully recovered.

In spite of Bill Clement's crusty ways, he proved to be a popular as well as a memorable governor. Steven Harrigan said of him, "Rip away Bill Clement's gruff, uncomplicated, free-enterprising public image and you'll find . . . a gruff, uncomplicated, free-enterprising kind of guy."

Bill Clements was truly a self-made man. He was confident and ambitious. When his second term of office ended, he decided to pull in his horns and return to private life. He and his wife Rita moved back to their home in Dallas, where they now live.

TEXAS TRIVIA AND TRUTH

Sam Rayburn served in the House of Representatives of the United States government for over forty-eight years.

Mark Wells White

There will be new faces and new ideas as a new generation of Texans prepare to take over the reins of government.

It is a generation that was educated after World War II — That grew up in the shadow of nuclear terror — That lived through our transition from a rural to an urban state — That watched towering buildings rise from the ground — That saw the first signs of progress choking our cities and despoiling our environment.

It is a generation whose time has come.

It is a generation whose hopes and visions and policies and actions will lead this state into the twenty-first century.

That is our destiny.

It is an exciting destiny for all of us.

Texas is the state of the future.

Mark Wells White
1983

MARK WELLS WHITE

JANUARY 18, 1983 TO JANUARY 20, 1987

Texas was in economic and political chaos. The state was suffering from a crisis of huge proportions. The oil industry was losing to international cartels. The commercial real estate industry was crashing. Banks and Savings and Loans were under federal attack and unemployment was at an all-time high. What, at one time, had made Texas great were now the contributing factors to its rapid, economic decline.

The Democratic party was no longer dominant. Voters spoke with a new voice. Blacks, Mexican Americans, and teachers insisted on being heard. No longer would they tolerate a *laissez-faire,* caretaker governor. Nor could they endure a multimillionaire ignoring their cries. Consequently, Mark White, the candidate with the least public baggage, squeaked by during the 1982 election to become the forty-first governor of Texas.

Mark White was born in Henderson, Texas, on March 17, 1940. His father was a shipfitter, his mother a schoolteacher. White's teenage years were spent in Houston, where he attended Lamar High School. As a Baptist, he attended Baylor University, graduating with both a business administration and a law degree. After passing the bar, he went to work for the attorney general's office in Austin and later moved to Houston, where he went into private practice with a Houston corporate law firm.

When Dolph Briscoe was governor, he invited Mark to become his secretary of state. This appointment proved to be valuable experience in Mark's political education. He was in charge of supervising the elections and the publication of state laws and statutes.

Later, he was appointed attorney general of the state. Here, his reputation suffered as he lost most of his cases. Unfortunately, this fact played a significant role when Mark decided to run for governor in the upcoming 1982 campaign.

Clements was running for reelection as a Republican. Mark White was the chosen candidate for the Democrats. The campaign trail was riddled with mudslinging and hot, negative assaults. Clements attacked White as a "bumbling incompetent." White, capitalized on Clements "meanness style" and criticized Clements for his lack of leadership. White pointed to the high utility rates, low teacher salaries, crisis in the water shortage, and rising interest rates that Clements had allowed.

Running as an underdog, with a heavy load of bad publicity, White shocked the voting public and won by a surprising margin. At forty-three years of age, he was the youngest man elected governor in almost half a century.

Immediately, both the Capitol and the governor took on a new image. Under Clements the office had a corporate look, says Paul Burka, but under White, ". . . women wear skirts and blouses, many men are in shirt sleeves, and the atmosphere comes close to the chaos of a political boiler room." The man, who had made little impact as secretary of state or attorney general, was forging ahead with astonishing administration skills.

Though his administration was a troubled one, White made enormous strides in his effort to appoint people of diverse backgrounds. He appointed a housewife to the Public Utility Commission. He appointed Mexican Americans and African Americans to other significant boards and agencies.

The hallmark of his administration was the Education Reform Act. This law raised teacher salaries, formed a teacher-testing program, limited class sizes, reduced teachers' paperwork, established a state-supported university research fund, and protected university budgets from constant cutbacks. The teachers' reactions were mixed. Some rebelled strongly against the teacher-testing program as well as White's support of Ross Perot's "no pass, no play" law. This law forbid students, who had failed any course during a six-week grading period, from participating in sports.

This disputable new law harmed White in another way. It carried with it a stiff tag in the form of a three-year $4.6 billion new tax package.

Texans, who persistently resisted high taxes, were not pleased. Grave economic conditions added to White's growing unpopularity. Though White fought off strong challengers in the primary in his bid for reelection, he found himself face-to-face with his former adversary, Bill Clements, in the general election.

Once again, campaign mud flew. Clements criticized White for his heavy spending program that went beyond the state's pay-as-you-go budget. White countered by accusing Clements of riding on the tail of President Reagan's popularity, whom, he declared, was responsible for the grim economic picture.

During such character bashing, White was forced to call a special session of the legislature to confront the budget deficit. It stood at $3.5 million, the largest state budgetary deficit in American history. Mark White could not withstand the negative publicity. Clements returned to the Capitol for the second time.

Many historians viewed Mark White's rise to fame as luck. Others disagreed. Like, Paul Burka, they felt that Mark White, "was the most substantive, most politically sophisticated governor of Texas since John Connally twenty years ago."

After his term of office, Mark White and his wife, Linda Gale, returned to private life in Houston.

TEXAS TRIVIA AND TRUTH

Texas has the largest and most diversified livestock industry in the United States.

Ann Willis Richards

Today, we have a vision of a Texas where opportunity knows no race or color or gender — a glimpse of the possibilities that can be when the barriers fall and the doors of government swing open. . . . we have a vision of a Texas with clean air and land and water . . . a Texas where strong economy is in harmony with a safe environment. . . . we have a vision of a Texas where every child receives an education that allows them to claim the full promise of their lives. . . . we have vision of a Texas where the government treats every citizen with respect and dignity and honesty . . . where consumers are protected . . . where businesses are nurtured and valued . . . where good jobs are plentiful . . . where those in need find compassion and help . . . where every decision is measured against a high standard of ethic and true commitment to public trust.

Tomorrow, we must build that Texas.

Ann Willis Richards
1991

ANN WILLIS RICHARDS

For two decades the Republican party had been making deeper and deeper inroads into Texas Democratic control. As the nineties emerged, there was a Republican in the White House, a Republican in the Statehouse, and a formidable Junior Republican Senator in the Senate. The can-do state was touting individualism in the face of a tradition that prided itself on a right-wing, conservative attitude about women. Cracks in the conservative concrete were becoming evident. Women were rapidly gaining presence as municipal office holders, mayors of large cities, and presidents of universities.

Additionally, Texas was on the verge of becoming the nation's second most populated state in the Union. Its gross national product was equal to that of 95 percent of the richest countries in the world. In spite of its larger-than-life image and recent economic downturn, Texas remained a strong component in the nation's political picture.

This was especially true at the Democratic National Convention in Atlanta in 1988. An unknown, Texas state official was chosen to deliver the keynote address. Ann Richards stood her full height of five feet, four inches and spit out a hard-hitting speech accented by a tart tongue and bawdy humor. Her memorable statement about President George Bush, "Poor George, he can't help it. He was born with a silver foot in his mouth," careened her into the national limelight.

Texas had a new rising star. Only this time it was a woman.

Dorothy Ann Willis was born on September 1, 1933, in Lakeview, Texas, a small community outside of Waco. She was the only child of Cecil and Iona Willis. As a school girl, she took piano and public speaking lessons, and she aspired to fulfill her father's admonition to accomplish whatever she set out to do. Remembered as a precocious child, she smoked hand-rolled cedar-bark cigars and one time attempted to fly off the garage roof like Superman.

For a short time during World War II, Ann lived with her parents in California, but returned to Waco to finish her high school education. She was active in sports, particularly basketball. She also excelled in English and speech. While in high school, she was selected to represent her school at Girls State, a mock government session sponsored by the Women's Auxiliary of the American Legion. From there she went to Washington, D.C., as one of her state's representative at the national convention.

After high school, Ann entered Baylor University on a speech scholarship, graduating with a degree in speech and political science. Later, she entered the University of Texas to earn a teacher's certificate.

For two years she taught government and history at Fulmore Junior High in Austin. In 1959, she and her husband David moved to Dallas. The next ten years Ann spent raising their four children and working as a volunteer in the Democratic party.

In 1969 the family returned to Austin, and in 1975 the local Democrats asked David Richards to run for county commissioner. He declined, but Ann, their second choice, agreed. Ann served as commissioner until she ran for and won the office of state treasurer. She was the first woman to hold a statewide office since "Ma" Ferguson.

Two personal problems were detrimental to Richard's campaign for governor — her divorce and her addiction to alcohol. Richards admits the divorce from her husband, David, was the hardest thing she had ever done. Her recovery and rehabilitation from alcohol has remained constant since 1981, but the ghost of it haunts her every day.

In the primary, two well-known opponents, Mark White, who desired to return to the Capitol, and Jim Maddox, the attorney general, ran against her. Barely edging them out in the primary, Ann was then faced in the general election with a newcomer to the political scene, Clayton Williams.

Williams had made his fortune in ranching, oil, and telecommunications. As a novice campaigner, he broke every campaign rule. Convinced he would win simply because he was a Republican, Williams disregarded the protocol of politics. His gaffs were rude, his speeches were off-color, and his refusal to shake hands with Richards sabotaged his efforts. The voting public was offended.

Ann Richards' victory in the gubernatorial race was, as many historians believe, a political accident. They believe that any other Republican beside Clayton Williams would have easily won.

Ann Richards, the first woman governor since "Ma" Ferguson, was now governor in her own right. Vowing to create a "New Texas," she proved to be a refreshing, hands-on administrator. She appointed many women, blacks, and Hispanics to state agencies and boards. She tackled sensitive issues such as lobbyist restrictions, the corrupt practices of the insurance board, and the controversial toxic waste disposal sites. It was definitely not "business as usual" in Austin.

Ann Richards, the feisty, handsome woman, with a white bouffant hairdo and a biting sense of humor, soon became the most popular governor in thirty years. She was the kind of person Texas needed in the 1990s — aggressive, tenacious, with a take-charge attitude. Halfway into her first term when asked by Paul Burka, in an interview for the *Texas Monthly* magazine, what she thought about being governor, she said, "I'm wiser, but sadder. I'm wiser because government is harder to change than I thought. I'm sadder because politics is a lot meaner than I thought."

No doubt, Ann Richards expressed the sentiment of every governor who presided over the great state of Texas during the twentieth century.

TEXAS TRIVIA AND TRUTH

March 7, 1986, Texas celebrated its sesquicentennial — a hundred and fifty years of independence.

George Walker Bush

Responsibility starts at home. It starts with responsible families. I wish I knew the law to cause people to love each other. I do not. But I do know our laws must be written to strengthen families, not diminish them. Every piece of legislation that crosses my desk will be judged by whether it keeps families together, safe and strong.

George Walker Bush
1995

GEORGE WALKER BUSH

JANUARY 17, 1995 –

On the national scene, politics, as it had been known in Washington, was crumbling under a forty-year reign of the Democratic party in Congress. Two years earlier a young Democrat had been elected president with an agenda for change, but the current dissatisfaction with the federal government crippled him from the start.

In Texas, while the economy was slowly but surely recovering from the economic set back of the 1980s, gang violence, street crimes, and drug trafficking were terrifying the citizens. In short, 1994 was a year of discontent.

Early in the year a young republican with a household name threw his hat into the Texas governor's race. It was a glaring, yet bold thing to do. Gov. Ann Richards was the most popular governor in over thirty years. She possessed a flamboyancy, a colorful language, and a charisma that Texans liked. To challenge her seemed futile, or more likely, politically suicidal. But George W. Bush was willing to take the risk and soon became a serious challenger.

Born on July 6, 1946, in New Haven, Connecticut, George was the first of five children born to future President George H. W. Bush and his wife Barbara.

Raised among wealth and privilege, young George grew up in Midland, Texas, where his father was in the oil business. As a young man, he was nicknamed the "Bombastic Bushkin" for he possessed a fun-loving nature, enjoying wild parties and beer busts, and often acting irreverent. His mother occasionally joked that he was the Bush black sheep.

After attending school in Midland, George enrolled in the exclusive prep school, Phillips Academy in Andover, Massachusetts, as his father had before him. Further following in his father's footsteps he went to Yale, where he majored in history. There he was elected president of his fraternity, Delta Kappa Epsilon. Unlike his father, who graduated Phi Beta Kappa, young George was no scholar, but he did manage a membership into the university's Skull and Bones Club, a secret society for the young men of prominent families.

After college, George W. returned to Houston, Texas, where he worked in an agribusiness. Considering this a dull, tedious job he shifted his interests and worked a year in an antipoverty program for the city. In 1973, after being rejected by the University of Texas School of Law, he applied and was accepted to the graduate program at Harvard Business School.

Two years later he returned to Midland and entered the oil business as a landsman working for day wages. It wasn't long before he started his own company, Arbusto, which is the Spanish word for "bush." Determined to make it on his own, he lived frugally and learned all he could about the oil business.

In 1977 he met and married Laura Welch, daughter of a Midland contractor. The following year he entered the 1978 race for the House of Representative. Winning the Republican primary against strong, negative publicity he then faced the popular Democratic state Senator Kent Hance from Lubbock in the general election. George Bush lost the race with 47 percent of votes compared to Hance's 53 percent, but his strong showing whet his appetite for politics. He quietly waited for future opportunity to again present himself politically.

Meanwhile, he centered his interests in the oil business. Changing his company's name to Bush Exploration, he began drilling for oil. Most of his funds were lost in dry holes, but in 1983, needing to recapitalize the company, he merged with Spectrum 7, an oil company out of

Cincinnati, Ohio. Later Spectrum 7 instigated a stock swap with Harken Energy of Dallas, keeping young George on their Corporate Board.

The Bushes then moved to Washington to help his father run for the presidency. After his father was elected, George W. brought his family back to Dallas. Always interested in baseball he began raising funds to purchase the Texas Rangers. As a bonus for putting the business deal together George W. was awarded 1.8 percent interest in the team and became their managing partner.

George considered running for governor of Texas in 1990, but decided against it as his father was still in office. When the president lost is bid for a second term, the time was ripe for George W. to enter the gubernatorial race.

George had learned a great deal about politics from his father, and he studied the minds and wishes of those, like himself, who were part of what was called the "Baby Boomers" of America. These were the children born after World War II. They were interested in more local control for the education of their children, safer streets, and relief from the welfare crunch caused, a great deal, by illegal aliens. Listening to them, George W. formed his "landscape for change" strategy which included an overhaul of the state's public education, welfare, and juvenile justice programs.

Campaigning with vigor, determination and a strong positive attitude, George spent six months criss-crossing the state with his highly-focused platform. Meanwhile, Governor Richards was attacking him personally and politically. She called him a "shrub" from the Bush tree. She hammered away at his inexperience as a businessman, and charged he was not a proven leader. Late in the campaign when the governor referred to Bush as a "jerk," Bush did not retaliate, but held to his positive line of campaigning. But the political atmosphere had changed.

By underestimating young George Bush's political abilities, his timing and his understanding of the Texas voter's desires, Richards lost the race, and young George W. became governor of Texas, January 17, 1995.

He and his wife, Laura, and their twin daughters, Barbara and Jenna, now live in Austin.

TEXAS TRIVIA AND TRUTH

In January 1989 the United States Department of Energy established the Superconductor Super Collider in Waxahachie. It was to be the biggest physics experiment ever performed. It was aborted by Congress in 1994.

BIBLIOGRAPHY

Ashmon, Charles. *Connally, The Adventures of Big John.* New York: William Morrow and Company, Inc., 1974.

Bolton, Paul. "Governors of Texas." *Corpus Christi Caller-Times,* 1947.

Brown, Norman W. *Hood, Bonnet and Little Brown Jug.* College Station: Texas A&M University Press, 1984.

Burka, Paul. "Sadder but Wiser," *Texas Monthly*, April, 1994.

Clark, James A. *The Tactful Texan, A Biography of Governor Will Hobby.* New York: Random House, 1958.

Conn, Jerry Douglas. *Preston Smith, The Making of a Texas Governor.* Austin: Pemberton Press, 1972.

Crawford, Ann Fears and Jack Keever. *John B. Connally, Portrait in Power.* Austin: Jenkins Press, 1973

Crawford, Ann Fears, Lorin Kennamer, and James V. Reese. *Texas, Lone Star Land.* Austin: W. S. Benson and Company, Inc., 1993.

Current Biographies. 1961, 1986, 1991. New York: H. W. Wilson Company.

DeBoer, Marvin E. Ed. *Destiny by Choice.* Fayetteville: University of Arkansas Press, 1992.

DeShields, James P. *They Sat in High Places.* San Antonio: Nayloc, 1940.

Dippel, Tieman. *The New Legacy.* Dallas: Taylor Publishing Co., 1988.

Fitzgerald, Hugh. "Governors I Have Known," *American Statesman,* 1927.

Frantz, Joe B. *Texas, A History.* New York: W. W. Norton and Company, Inc., 1984.

Gantt, Fred. *The Chief Executive in Texas, A Study in Gubernatorial Leadership.* Austin: University of Texas Press, 1964.

Governors of Texas, Texas Almanac, Dallas Morning News, Dallas, Texas, 1992.

Green, George Norris. *The Establishment in Texas Politics, The Primitive Years, 1938–1957.* Norman: University of Oklahoma Press, 1979.

Haley, James L. *Texas From Spindletop Through World War II.* New York: St. Martin's Press, 1993.

Hollandsworth, Skip. "George W. Bush." *Texas Monthly,* Austin, May 1994.

Hollard, T. A., and Violet M. Robert. *The Double Log Cabin, History of Parker County.* Weatherford: Herald Publishing, 1937.

Ivins, Molly. *Molly Ivins Can't Say That, Can She?* New York: Random House, 1991.

Kraemer, Richard and Charldean Newell. *Essentials of Texas Politics.* St. Paul: West Publishing, 1986.

Kinch, Sam and Stuart Long. *Allan Shivers, The Pied Piper of Texas Politics.* Austin: Shoal Creek, 1973.

Lubbock, Francis. *Six Decades in Texas.* Austin: Pemberton Press, 1968.

McComb, David G. *Texas, A Modern History.* Austin: University of Texas Press, 1989.

McCleskey, Butcher, and Stephens Farlow. *The Government and Politics of Texas, Seventh Edition.* Boston: Little Brown & Company, 1982.

McKay, Seth S. and Odie B. Faulk. *Texas After Spindletop.* Austin: Steck-Vaughn Company, 1965.

McKay, Seth S. *W. Lee O'Daniel and Texas Politics.* Lubbock: Texas Tech Press, 1944.

McDonald, Archie P. *Texas, A History.* New York: W. W. Norton & Company, Inc., 1984.

Mooney, Booth. *Mister Texas, A Story of Coke Stevenson.* Dallas: Texas Printing House, 1947.

Moore, Walter. "Governors of Texas." *Dallas Morning News,* 1964.

Morehead, Richard. *50 Years in Texas Politics.* Austin: Eakin Press, 1982.

Morris, Celia. *Storming the Statehouse*. New York: Charles Schribner Sons, 1992.

Nalle, Ouida Ferguson. *The Fergusons of Texas or "Two Governors for the Price of One."* San Antonio: Naylor Press, 1946.

Neff, Pat M. *The Battles of Peace, an Autobiography*. Fort Worth: Pioneer, 1925.

Olien, Roger M. *From Token to Triumph*. Dallas: Southern Methodist University Press, 1982.

Perry, George Sessions. *Texas, A World in Itself.* Gretna: Pelican Publishing Company, 1975.

Pittman, H. C. *Inside the Third House*. Austin: Eakin Press, 1992.

Political Profiles, The Nixon/Ford Years. New York: Facts on File, Inc., 1979.

Pringle, David. *Texas Monthly Political Reader, 3rd Edition*. Austin.

Reston, James, Jr. *The Lone Star, The Life of John Connally.* New York: Harper & Row, 1989.

Richards, Ann. *Straight from the Heart*. New York: Simon & Schuster, 1989.

Richardson, Rupert. *Texas, The Long Star State*. Englewood Cliffs: Prentice Hall, 1943, 1970, 1988.

Shirley, Emma Morrell. *Administration of Pat Neff, Governor of Texas*. Waco: Baylor University, 1938.

Stone, Ron. *The Book of Texas Days*. Fredericksburg: Shearer Publishing, 1984.

Welch, June Rayfield. *The Governors of Texas*. Dallas: GLA Press, 1977.

Whisenhunt, Donald W. *Texas, A Sesquicentennial Celebration*. Austin: Eakin Press, 1984.

Wyatt, Fredeorica and Shelton Hooper. *Coke R. Stevenson, A Texas Legend*. Junction: Shelton Press, 1976.

Index